Guide *to your* Parenting Concerns

- Chores • Communication • Cooperation
- Discipline • Divorce • Holidays • Homework
- Marriage • Morality • Setting Limits • Sexuality
- Sharing • Step-Parenting • Stress • Teen-agers
- Toddlers ... and much more

by Linda Lewis Griffith, M.A., M.F.C.C.

Kindred Books
P. O. Box 4818
San Luis Obispo, CA 93403

Copyright © 1996 Kindred Books. All rights reserved. No part of this book may be reproduced or transmitted in any form or by any means, electronic or mechanical, including photocopying, recording, or by any information storage and retrieval system without written permission from the publisher, except for the inclusion of brief quotations in a review.

First Printing 1996

Cover design by Vicki Douras, Vail, Colorado

ISBN Number: 0-9648933-0-4

Library of Congress Catalog Card Number: 95-95128

Printed and bound in the United States of America.

To Christine, Jim, Anno, Shelton and Diane.

You never stopped believing.

L. L. G.

Contents

Preface i

Chapter

1   **Raising Great Kids**   1

- Classy Kids   2
- Raising Responsible Children   5
- Teaching Good Manners To Your Youngsters   8
- Building Your Children's Self-Esteem   11
- Building Respect   14
- Developing Honest Children   17
- Raising Independent Children   20
- Chores   22
- Developing Competence In Your Youngsters   25
- Teaching Kids To Make Good Decisions   28
- Boredom Has A Place In Children's Lives   31
- Kids And Money   34
- Talking To Your Children About Sex   37

2   **Discipline**   40

- 10 Common Discipline Mistakes   41
- Constructive Alternatives To Punishment   44
- Clear Parenting   47
- Pre-Praising Your Children   50
- Praise   53
- Learning To Say "No" To Your Youngsters   55
- Enlist Your Youngsters' Help In Solving Problems   58
- Don't Fall Prey To Childish Antics   61

3 Strong Families 64

- Characteristics Of Strong Families 65
- Special Moments 68
- Family Dinners 70
- Assuming Leadership In Your Home 73
- Nurturing Spirituality In Your Family 76
- Let Your Children Know You Love Them 79
- There's No "Right Way" To Raise Children 82
- Family Celebrations 85
- Expectations For Your Youngsters 88
- Titles Of Respect 91
- Humor 94
- Sibling Camaraderie 97
- Birth Order Helps Define Who We Are 100

4 How We Talk To Our Children... And How Our Children Talk To Us 103

- Improving Your Family's Communication 104
- Lecturing 107
- Rude Language Has No Place In Your Household 110
- Name-Calling 113
- Overtalking 116
- Silencing Your Youngsters' Whining 119
- Breaking Kids' Interrupting Habits 122
- Stop Nagging Your Kids 125
- Kicking Kids' Bad-Word Habits 128
- Parental Self-Talk 131
- Talking With Your Youngsters 134

5	**Stress and Anxiety**	**137**
	• Stress	138
	• Fast-Lane Families	141
	• Beating The "Way-Too-Much-To-Do Blues"	144
	• Kicking The Rush-Rush Routine	147
	• Morning Mayhem	150
	• Taking Five	153
	• Guilt	156
	• Helping Children Manage Their Anger	159
	• Hovering	162
	• Don't Overdo For Your Kids	165
	• Helping Your Children Manage Frustration	168
	• Teaching Kids About Safety	171
	• Managing Children's Varying Time Demands	174
	• When You're A Less-Than-Perfect Parent	177
6	**School Work and Education**	**180**
	• Raising Smart Children	181
	• Your Children's Education	184
	• You Can Improve Your Child's Education	187
	• School Work	190
	• Turn Off The TV And Turn On Your Children's Minds	193
	• Let's Support Our Public Schools	196
	• Parent-Teacher Conferences	199
	• Reading Aloud To Your Children	201
	• Helping Kids Establish Sound Homework Habits	204

7	**Challenging Children**	**207**
	• Managing Your Difficult-To-Like Child	208
	• Helping Kids Cope With Their Own Personalities	211
	• Facts About A. D. D.	214
	• Different Drummers	217
	• Sensitive Children Need Extra TLC	220
	• Bedwetting	223
	• Helping Kids Cope With Nightmares	226
	• When Children Pick Friends You Don't Like	229
	• When Children Want To Run Away From Home	232
8	**Marriage**	**235**
	• Successful Marriages	236
	• Managing Long-Distance Marriages	239
	• An Important Note To Mothers	242
9	**Divorce And Blended Families**	**245**
	• Divorce	246
	• Blending Families Together	249
	• Managing Your Ex-Spouse's New Relationship	252
	• Dispelling Myths About Divorce	255
10	**From Pregnancy To Pre-School**	**258**
	• Deciding If You Want To Have Children	259
	• Preparing For Your New Arrival	262
	• Preparing Siblings For New Baby's Arrival	265
	• Macho Motherhood	268
	• Acknowledging Life's Stages	271

	• Sharing	274
	• Shopping With Your Youngsters	277
11	**Teens And Adolescents**	280
	• Making Good Decisions	281
	• Teen-age Sexual Abstinence	284
	• Teen Dating	287
12	**Grandparents And Grandchildren**	290
	• Custodial Grandparents	291
	• Managing Visiting Grandchildren	294
13	**Violence And Gangs**	296
	• Steps For Minimizing Childhood Violence	297
	• Discouraging Children from Joining Gangs	300
14	**Sports And Family Fitness**	303
	• Fit Kids, Healthy Kids	304
	• Don't Rush Children Into Sports	307
	• Coaching Your Youngster In Sports	310
	• Fitting Fitness Into Your Family	313
15	**Happy Holidays**	316
	• Handling The Holidays	317
	• The Value Of Holiday Traditions	320
	• Surviving Holiday Relatives	323
	• Thank You Notes	326
	• Teaching Kids About Giving	329
	• Buying Children's Toys	332

Preface

My life is devoted to children and families. Not only do I have a long-standing marriage and two pre-teen kids of my own, but my counseling practice centers around helping parents manage their youngsters more effectively.

A lot has been written about the problems of so-called dysfunctional families. Alcoholism, child abuse and incest are hot topics for magazines, talk shows and best-sellers. But I like to assist everyday moms and dads in tackling the humdrum scenarios they face. Bedwetting, lying, chores, respect, bad attitude and name-calling never make it to the headlines. Yet parents in the child-rearing trenches grapple with these and bigger foes as a matter of course.

Problems with kids can be insurmountable. Mothers and fathers don't know where to begin in looking for workable solutions. And, as issues piggyback onto other issues, it's easy to get lost in the fog. For example, a boy's poor homework habits can be made worse by difficulties paying attention to his teacher, and these can be magnified by his parents' arguing at home.

The key is to simplify each problem into a clear-cut, "oh-now-I-get-it" format. It's imperative to sort out extraneous information and zero in on one, manageable issue at a time. Then, after you know what you are trying to solve, you can select a few easy-to-follow solutions. Is the problem getting your daughter to sleep in her own bed? Try these three ideas. Not sure how to stop your son's bad-word habit? Here are four suggestions.

Of course, not all dilemmas can be resolved one-two-three. They are far too complex to respond to instant solutions. But diligently following a distinct game plan with your family's challenges goes much further toward seeking answers than wallowing in a bog of uncertainty.

The topics covered in *Guide To Your Parenting Concerns* are collections of my national parenting column which is carried by the Scripps-Howard News Service. They range from teen-age sexuality to sibling rivalry, communication to custodial grandparents, divorce to attention deficit. Each item attempts to define a specific situation, then offers suggestions every parent can follow. Solutions are based on my training as a family therapist, current research in the parenting field, experiences from clients in my counseling practice, input from parents attending talks and lectures, and my on-the-job training as a wife and mother.

I am indebted to the late Jeff Fairbanks and the staff of the *Telegram-Tribune* who helped me develop my weekly column from a casual, "let's-give-it-a-try" idea, to an article now available to over 600 newspapers nationwide.

And I want to extend my deepest appreciation to Dr. Harvey Levenson, whose support and tireless effort with this project have gone far beyond his original offer to help me organize my material into a book, and have resulted in the final product you now hold in your hand.

L. L. G.

Chapter 1

•

Raising Great Kids

"Fine manners need the support of fine manners in others."

Ralph Waldo Emerson
1803-1882

Classy Kids
*Treasures to Themselves and
Those Around Them*

Classy Kids are children who are respectful of others and have a strong sense of right and wrong. They are considerate and cooperative. In short, they're a pleasure to be around.

Classy Kids come from all different backgrounds. Some are from affluent homes, others from families who barely make ends meet. Some are top students, others struggle with their school work. Their parents may be married or divorced. They may be only children or one of many. The common factor is that they are highly moral youngsters who work well with those around them.

Classy Kids are certainly not perfect. They sometimes forget their homework, or squabble with their sisters. Their beds may be a jumble of covers, and they may grumble when it's their turn to feed the family pet.

What they're not likely to be guilty of, however, is talking rudely to a teacher, bullying their classmates, or vandalizing school property. Their flaws are mostly issues of maturation, not problems of respect.

Classy Kids are hardly robots. Rather, they are usually well liked by their fellow students and confident in their abilities. They relate to both youngsters and adults. They trust themselves to handle new situations.

Classy Kids are made, not born. Every child has the potential to become one. Sure, all children relate to their worlds with unique styles. And some boys and girls arrive with personalities that interact more easily with their environments than others.

But, since the values of respect and cooperation are instilled as children grow, every youngster has the capability of earning the title, Classy.

How do you do it? Start by initiating a zero-tolerance policy for all rudeness, lack of respect and poor language. Whether your toddler calls you "Stupid," or your thirteen year-old uses foul language on the tennis court, your response should be the same: state clearly that the behavior is not acceptable, and that you want it stopped.

Set high standards of behavior for your children. Let them know they are too intelligent, successful or motivated to be rude or disrespectful. Honest statements such as, "Janine, you're such a bright, classy girl. I know you can behave differently toward your brother," reinforce her self-esteem while establishing limits on her behavior.

Enforce the same standards for other youngsters in your presence. I know it can feel uncomfortable, but don't be afraid to let your kids' friends know when they're out of line.

Let's say your son and his friend are in the back seat of the car, and the friend tells an off-color joke. Politely tell the boy, "Joe, we don't talk like that in our home." Should Joe persist in being rude, he will simply not be welcome at your house.

Discuss examples of appropriate behavior with your children. Analyze how those behaviors look, sound and feel to others. For instance, you might say, "Have you noticed how Sarah always checks with her mother when she wants to stay and play? That's a considerate thing to do."

Praise your children when they demonstrate top-notch behavior. When your daughter offers to baby-sit for her younger sister while you go out for the evening, reinforce her cooperation with a heartfelt, "Hey, I really appreciate your thoughtfulness. You're one terrific girl."

Model cooperative, respectful behavior at home. For example, avoid name-calling, put-downs, insults or profanity. Learn positive methods of discipline. And use constructive ways to solve family problems.

Classy Kids don't develop overnight. They take years of nurturing, commitment, patience and perseverance to mature. But they're definitely worth the effort. These competent individuals will be an asset to themselves, their families and their communities for years to come.

Raising Responsible Children

Want to raise responsible children? Start with these guidelines:

Start early. Kids are never too young to learn responsibility. Have them perform routine tasks suitable to their ages and abilities. A pre-schooler can help feed a family pet. A three year-old can unload silverware from the dishwasher. They'll love helping out and they'll be learning their first lessons about being responsible.

Explain your expectations to your child. Let your youngsters know what steps they need to perform in order to behave responsibly. Perhaps when your son does the dishes, you want him to load the dishwasher, clean off the counter tops, and fold the dish towels before he leaves the kitchen. When your daughter borrows the car, you expect she will return it with a full tank of gas, and no trash on the floor. Too often we expect our kids to read our minds instead of telling them what we want them to do.

Practice your expectations with your child. Let's say son Toby, age eight, has a new kitten. To responsibly care for that pet you want him to feed and water it daily, and to clean its litterbox twice a week. The first day the kitten's home, you take Toby through each step of what he'll need to do for his pet. You continue practicing throughout the next few weeks.

Review your expectations for responsible behavior with your child. Until responsibility becomes a habit, you'll have to remind your kids about how they are to behave. Gentle reminders such as, "Don't forget to stop by and see Grandma after school," help your child learn to behave in a responsible manner.

These reminders are *not* to be confused with nagging. Nagging is something you say repeatedly without any change in the child's behavior. Parents feel angry and ignored; kids wish they had cotton for their ears. If you find yourself on the nag wagon, go to the next step:

Problem-solve stumbling blocks. If there's an area where your youngster repeatedly acts irresponsibly, have a problem-solving session. Ask your child to come up with solutions that will ensure similar future problems will be avoided. If a child repeatedly forgets his lunch, ask him what he can do to make sure he remembers it. Perhaps he needs to place it by the front door, or put it in his backpack before he eats his breakfast. Avoid solving the problem for him. Let him come up with his own solutions.

Praise responsible behavior. A sincere, "Thanks, Trish. That was responsible to wait for your brother before crossing the street," lets them know you appreciate their responsible actions. We all like to know we've done a good job. Behaving responsibly is no exception.

Let kids experience the consequences of their irresponsibility. If you bail them out of their problems, you're keeping them from taking responsibility for themselves. I no longer remind my two boys when it's time for them to leave for school. If they're tardy, they'll have to suffer the consequences. When your daughter forgets to return the car in time, she loses the privilege of using the car for the rest of the week. If a son has trouble remembering to bring his baseball mitt to practice, he'll have to go without it.

<u>Be firm. Don't back down when they scream, plead or sulk.</u> Our job as parents is to teach our kids to be responsible, not to win popularity contests. Sure, they're apt to be angry when we ignore their cries for help. But the sooner kids learn they're the only ones responsible for what happens in their lives, the sooner they'll start taking responsibility for themselves.

Teaching Good Manners To Your Youngsters

I'm a stickler for good manners. I like children to say "Please" and "Thank you," to shake hands when they are introduced to new people, and to generally show consideration for others.

Why teach kids good manners? The most obvious reason is they're more pleasant to be around. Other parents, teachers, scout leaders, and even other youngsters, prefer spending time with polite kids.

Manners teach children our culture's rules for dealing with everyday situations. Children gain confidence in their knowledge of how to handle themselves in new settings. And well-mannered boys and girls are more likely to be included in activities than their less controlled classmates.

Good manners lost favor during the seventies and early eighties. They were associated with rigid child-raising practices, and were accused of stifling a child's personal development. Child-rearing books with the word "Free" in their titles were as common as VW vans. Setting limits on kids was taboo.

Fortunately, manners are back in vogue. And, though they aren't difficult to teach youngsters, they don't happen by themselves. Parents hoping to instill their kids with social graces must commit themselves to the ongoing process.

Here's how you do it:

Begin by selecting one situation and deciding how you want your child to behave. For example, you might decide that when your daughter answers the phone, you'd like her to say, "Hello, this is Mandy." If the call is for someone else, you'd like her to respond, "Just a moment, please. I'll go get my mother."

Next, gently explain to Mandy how you'd like her to answer the phone. Pick a time when she can focus on what you're saying; don't do it as you're rushing out the door, or lecturing her about something else

Third, encourage all members of the family to use good manners. Treat each other respectfully. Thank your spouse for stopping by the store before dinner, for instance, or remember to say "Please" when asking your son to take out the recycling.

Practice the desired manners often. Good manners are a habit, and must be repeated until they are automatic. When teaching your daughter to answer the phone politely, you might have her practice on a toy phone several times until she does it correctly. Perhaps a grandparent can call at a pre-arranged time, so she can hone her skill even further.

Review good manners regularly. Before entering a restaurant, remind your kids of the manners you expect. Before you take your child into the library, review how he is to behave inside the building. I would sometimes add a touch of humor when reviewing good manners with my own boys. Before entering the library, I would say, "Now remember, I want you to yell and run around when we're in the library." They would laugh and giggle at that suggestion because they had already learned the *real* rules.

Gently correct your children if their manners aren't up to par. Remind them of the appropriate behavior. Never honor a child's request if it has been made rudely. Instead, explain that as soon as good manners have been used, you'll be happy to consider it.

Finally, sincerely praise your children when they've displayed good manners. An admiring smile, a pat on the head or a warm statement are great reinforcers. I also enjoy sharing the remarks of others. Such statements as, "Mr. Collins told me that he was so impressed with your polite manners when you were at his house. We're really proud of your behavior," let them know they're on the right track.

Building Your Children's Self-Esteem

Self-esteem is a belief in oneself. Below are five factors for developing self-esteem in children.

<u>COMPETENCE</u>. Competence, or mastery, means children feel in control of themselves and their surroundings. For example, a two year-old gains mastery over her environment by having a step stool that enables her to reach the sink to wash her hands without assistance.

A ten year-old gains physical competence as he learns to throw a football with his parent or friends.

A third-grader develops psychological competence when he learns how to handle the playground bully.

Encouraging children to feel in control does not mean children control the family. Rather, it means kids learn how to take care of themselves as much as they are able, and to solve their own problems without external help.

<u>RESPECT</u>. Children develop respect for themselves when they are respected by other members of their families. Parents show respect for their youngsters in a variety of ways. They can use polite words and phrases when addressing their sons and daughters.

They can be aware of their children's levels of development and understand age-appropriate behaviors.

They can recognize different patterns of learning and academic achievement, offering support at each level of success.

Parents do not show respect for their kids whenever they are hitting, yelling at or belittling them.

CHALLENGES. Children who are provided regular, appropriate challenges expand their levels of competence by attempting--and mastering--new skills. They feel good about themselves and their abilities.

Youngsters who are not challenged not only fail to recognize their potentials, but miss out on feeling successful.

Challenges may be physical, such as learning how to throw a bounce pass or bake cookies. Or they may be emotional, such as learning how to handle a homework problem with a teacher.

Challenges should be motivating, not discouraging or overwhelming. Parents should keep an eye open to gauge their youngsters' levels of frustration.

For instance, reading material that may challenge and excite one first grader may frustrate her classmate to the point of tears.

LIMITS. Limits and structure provide kids with clear guidelines from which to operate their lives. Limits mean fewer decisions and less confusion.

We set limits for our youngsters whenever we tell them how to behave. "No running in the house," or "You need to be home by five o'clock," give concise directives about what we want from them.

Of course, our kids will push against these same structures with disgusted looks, sighs of contempt or tantrums.

But limits are actually comforting for children. Youngsters without adequate structure often feel out of control and lacking in guidance.

SUPPORT. The process of building self-esteem is a bumpy one. Children need lots of nurturing and support as they tackle new skills and develop strategies for coping with their lives.

Encouraging words, such as, "I know you'll do great on that test," instill confidence. Wise words, such as, "Let's see what we can do to make this water glass easier for you to reach," teach problem-solving skills. And understanding words, such as, "I know that didn't feel good at the doctor's office. Let's cuddle up and read a good story together," offer security in the knowledge there is nothing our children can't handle.

Building Respect

To respect someone means to value or show consideration for that person.

We can respect our children in a variety of ways. For example, we can seriously listen to their problems and fears, then encourage them to find solutions. We can be considerate of their bodies as we change their diapers, bathe them or treat a medical condition. We can use polite words when we speak to them.

Children can respect adults by addressing them as "Mr." or "Mrs.", or by using other titles of respect. They can use polite words and phrases. They can follow directions. They can assist adults as needed.

Parents and children do not respect each other whenever hitting, name-calling, yelling, screaming, talking-back, or insulting behavior is involved.

Respect is vital to families because it lays the groundwork for members to care about and value one another. When people are valued by others, they feel more valuable themselves. Self-esteem and confidence soar.

Respect also provides a structure for relating to others and reaching mutually acceptable conclusions. When problems are solved with respect, both parties are more likely to feel pleased with the outcome. When problems are solved without respect, one person is likely to feel angry, hurt or taken advantage of.

Unfortunately, disrespectful behavior seems to be in vogue. Television and movies abound in portraying rude and aggressive youngsters who delight in insulting their parents and neighbors. Name-calling and foul language have become the norm rather than the exception on such programs. Concern for others' property seems non-existent.

You can help reverse this trend. Start by giving respect a high priority in your home. There is no time when disrespect is appropriate in a family setting.

Speak respectfully to all members of the family.

Let's say your teen-age daughter wants to go to an unsupervised party. A disrespectful response might be, "Of all the hair-brained ideas you've come up with. I can't believe you'd be stupid enough to think I'd let you go!" A more respectful response might be, "I know you'd like to go, but I'm uncomfortable with the fact that no adults will be present. I'm sorry, but this time you'll have to stay home."

Learn to discipline with respect. For instance, if your tot continually drops food from his high chair, calmly lift him out and explain, "We're all done eating," rather than slap his hand.

In another instance, if your fourth grader is doing poorly on his spelling tests, try problem-solving rather than grounding or humiliating him. You'll be helping him develop strategies for tackling difficult subjects without damaging his self-esteem.

Get out of the name-calling and put-down habit. Since the purpose is to build mutual respect in the family, insulting others is never OK.

Use liberal doses of "Please" and "Thank you" around the house. You'll be instilling excellent manners as well as boosting morale.

Limit your kids' exposures to disrespectful kinds of media. You'll teach your children there are better programs to watch, and you'll send a message to the producing studios that you and your family don't support the current trends.

Finally, be prepared for the inevitable response, "But Mom and Dad...everybody else can watch (or do or say) that. Why can't I?" The simple truth is not everybody else can watch or do or say disrespectful things. You have the authority to determine which behaviors are not allowed in your home. Be firm and don't cave in.

Developing Honest Children

All parents want their children to tell the truth. We want to know we can trust them when they tell us where they've been, what they've done, or whom they've been with.

Unfortunately, many of us unwittingly encourage our kids to be dishonest. We frighten or intimidate them into the very act we dread most--lying.

Below are seven steps to help you foster honesty in your family. The goal is not to eradicate every falsehood, but rather to develop relationships that increase the likelihood of honesty.

Step #1: Create an atmosphere of honesty in your home. Show your children that you value telling the truth by being honest with them, your spouse and other people in your life. If, for example, you lie regularly to your husband, it's easier for your kids to lie to you. Even an innocent lie, such as directing your child to tell an unwelcome caller you're not home, establishes a pattern of dishonesty.

Step #2: Make sure your young child knows what a lie is, and how it differs from fantasy. Explain to preschoolers that a lie is when they know what really happened but tell you something different. Fantasy, or pretending, is when you both know it never happened. Let them know that there are fun times to pretend, but there are other times when it is important to tell the truth.

Step #3: Expect honesty from your children. Tell your youngsters that you always want them to tell you the truth, and that you will always be honest with them.

Step #4: Assume that your son or daughter is telling the truth. Let them know that you will believe what they say, and you will continue to believe them as long as they have not given you reason to doubt them. As soon as they have broken their trust, they will have to reestablish it again. It's important to allow them to rebuild their trust; growing up is a learning process, not a final decree.

Step #5: Don't ask your child a question if you already know the answer. You'll be encouraging that child to lie to save face. Let's say your pre-schooler has climbed into the kitchen cupboard and spilled flour all over the floor. When you arrive upon the scene, finding your tot elbow-deep in powder, your first reaction may be to shriek, "Matthew, did you do this?" Most likely, Matt will look up from the dust and mutter a feeble, "No." Instead, respond,"UH-oh, I see we've got a mess on our hands. Come on, Matt, help me clean this up."

Step #6: Don't make the consequences of telling the truth worse than lying. If, for example, you storm into the house and demand to know who borrowed your car and dented the front fender so you can personally throttle him, you're likely to be met with denial. Who's going to admit to an act they know will result in an explosion? Instead, try to calmly discuss what happened with your family: "It seems that somebody used the car without my permission, and now the car is dented. I won't be angry, but I would like to know who took it, so we can work out some kind of arrangement to get it fixed."

Step #7: Always reward your children for telling the truth, even if you don't approve of the behavior they're telling you about. Let's face it, kids are going to make mistakes, and we want them to come to us for guidance when they do.

Here's what I mean: Your high school junior calls you from a party, saying she has had too much to drink, and could you please come and pick her up. You didn't know alcohol was even going to be served at the party and, although you're angry and disappointed that she did this, you are glad she has told you the truth and made a wise decision about getting home. Save the lecture for later. Support her honesty now.

Raising Independent Children

"Children seem more dependent than before," an experienced first-grade teacher recently told me.

This twenty year veteran observed that boys and girls in her classes needed more supervision in completing their school work, and showed more signs of frustration, such as crying or refusing to participate, when they couldn't master a simple task. "Parents aren't teaching their kids to be independent," she sighed.

Independent children feel confident to make decisions and take actions on their own without needing help from adults. They also possess the social skills that enable them to act on their own.

Here's what I mean: Tammy is an independent five year-old who can go to a friend's house after kindergarten. She is confident about her ability to be away from her mother for several hours. She can take care of herself in most situations, but is also comfortable asking her playmate's mother for assistance getting a drink of water, or pulling a game down from a closet. Tammy feels secure and safe in a variety of new environments.

Lisa, also in Tammy's class, is more dependent. She is afraid to play with friends after school, and cries if her mother doesn't stay with her. She is afraid of new situations; she doesn't feel confident to solve problems by herself.

Once, when Lisa spilled juice on her shirt while at a friend's house, she cried until her mother could come and get her, rather than wear a similar blouse from her friend's closet.

Certainly, some youngsters are born with outgoing personalities while others are naturally more withdrawn. But there are steps parents can take to foster independence in their tots.

Start by praising and supporting your children's efforts to be independent. Statements such as, "You made a good decision to return that wallet to its owner," or "Bringing me that knife you found on the playground shows me you're a responsible person," let youngsters know they can be in control of new situations and show good judgment.

When kids don't show good judgment, avoid making them feel bad. Let them know they've made a mistake, then discuss better actions for next time.

Instill respect, not fear, of the outside world. Much attention has been recently focused on child abduction and sexual molestation. While we want our children to know how to avoid dangerous situations, we don't want them to be paralyzed by fear. The actual odds of being kidnapped are very slight. The odds of frightening youngsters into incompetence are much, much greater.

Provide safe opportunities for your tots to practice independence. For example, give your son a dollar to select a treat, then let him pay for it at the check-out counter by himself. Or encourage your daughter to order her own meal in a restaurant. You'll be there to back them up, but, most importantly, you'll be there to support their success at gaining mastery of their world.

Chores
An Integral Part of Your Children's Lives

Do your children have enough chores? Many of today's kids don't. And unfortunately they're worse off because of it.

Chores are regular household duties that youngsters perform without being paid. A ten year-old may mow the lawn, a teen may do the laundry or wash the family car. Even a pre-schooler may help feed a pet or set the table.

Chores are important for kids for a number of reasons. First, they teach responsibility. Because chores are a necessity for a smooth running household, youngsters learn they have to do them before they go to scouts or play with friends.

Chores foster a sense of belonging. When every family member pitches in to make things happen, each feels that he or she is an integral part of the family unit.

Chores teach youngsters how to work for the betterment of a group, rather than solely for themselves. Kids put the needs of the family before their own, and learn to be less self-centered.

Chores develop self-esteem. Kids feel important when they can proudly assert, "This family couldn't manage without me."

Chores teach competence and mastery. When a boy learns how to change a washer in a leaky faucet, and his sister masters the art of pruning a fruit tree, they have acquired valuable skills that will assist them throughout their lives.

Rural societies didn't have to worry if their children had adequate numbers of chores. Tending gardens, maintaining farm equipment, and raising livestock kept kids busy from morning until night.

But as families have moved to urban neighborhoods, condominiums and apartments, household responsibilities have dwindled. Time once spent doing chores has too often become time spent hanging around malls. Rural responsibilities have devolved into Main Street monotony.

I'm not saying we should all move back to the farm, or that children should spend every waking moment at hard labor. What I am encouraging parents to do, however, is to make sure their kids have enough responsibilities at home, and they're reaping the benefits that go with them.

How many chores should kids have? I recommend a minimum 30 minutes of daily responsibilities, and at least one or two hours on the weekends. Of course, this is an average. One weekend your family may work for hours cleaning out the garage or hauling clippings, and the next weekend take a trip to the lake.

Spend time teaching children what you want them to do. Youngsters aren't born knowing how to start the washing machine or how to load the wood box. Work with them the first few times they try it, then keep a watchful eye from a distance.

Avoid being too picky about your kids' workmanship. Sure, you want them to do the job correctly. But don't expect your first-grader to set the table perfectly, or your fifth-grader to mow the lawn like a pro. Keeping realistic standards will insure that your children want to help, and that everyone feels satisfied with the outcome.

Make chores more enjoyable for your children by letting them pick which ones are theirs. Make a list of what needs to get done, then let each child choose. Of course, there will be those nobody wants; rotate them often so no one gets stuck.

Finally, avoid making chores a chore (excuse the pun). Let's face it, they're part of life. Instead, instill in your kids the value that working together can be fun. Teach your children how to accomplish their tasks with a good attitude, then move on to other parts of their day.

Developing Competence In Your Youngsters

Competence is a mastery of the skills appropriate at each developmental stage of our children's lives. Whether they're learning to tie their shoes, ride a bicycle, mow the lawn or drive a car, competence is a primary goal.

Kids experience competence at different levels. Babies first strive for physical competence. They learn to crawl and walk, feed themselves and use the toilet. Children gain social competence. They get along with friends, know how to share their toys, and learn how to ask for assistance. Youngsters develop academic competence by learning to write their names, read, take spelling tests and write a term paper.

Competence not only helps children master their environments, but boosts their psychological development as well. For instance, competence builds kids' self-esteem. Learning how to do things makes them feel confident of their abilities and feel good about themselves. This confidence spreads to other areas of their lives, increasing their willingness to learn new skills or venture into unknown situations.

How can you encourage competence in your children? Start by creating an environment that supports their efforts towards mastery. Allow tots plenty of time to learn how their bodies and lives work. Give them space to be messy and to explore. Provide them the necessary tools, such as crayons, colored paper, blocks, shovels and buckets, with which to experiment, design and build.

Avoid phrases such as, "Here, let me do it," and "You never do anything right." Replace them with, "You can do it," or "Look how you're doing that yourself!"

Be patient. I know our days can feel hectic. And we're often pulled in six directions at once. But a toddler's job is to slowly gain competence. That requires all his concentration. Instead of hurrying, try to sit back, relax and enjoy his strivings for success.

Teach kids skills and strategies for developing competence in various areas. You can show your daughter how to write the letters of her name. You can demonstrate to your second-grader how to crack an egg into a bowl. You can discuss with your Girl Scout how to sell cookies door to door. Break each skill into small, easily manageable segments, then gently explain the steps to your child.

Practice competence with your children. Give them lots of opportunities to become proficient in the skills they are acquiring. For example, allow your youngsters to check their own books out of the library. Or have your child assist you in the kitchen so he learns to cook. I know, it often takes longer to have them do things than to handle them ourselves. But the goal is to develop competence in our children, not shave moments off our schedules.

When my young sons want to make large purchases, such as aquariums or stereos, we visit various retailers so they can discuss what they want with the salespeople. They compare prices, analyze values, and make informed decisions about their purchases. Of course, this takes lots of time. And it would be much easier for me to buy the items for them. But the competence and self-confidence they gain in the process are invaluable. It's worth every second we spend shopping.

Encourage their progress towards competence. Support their efforts, not just their successes. Hug your second-grader who's struggling to learn his sight words. Comfort the bruised egos encountered by your toddler as she attempts those first steps. Empathize with your ninth-grader as he tackles Algebra. Warmly acknowledge the would-be cheerleader who practices tirelessly to make the squad. Rave with your grade-schooler in his attempts to conquer the latest trick on his skateboard.

Finally, celebrate their mastery. Praise her acceptance on the Pep Squad. Laud his memorization of his spelling list. Cheer her success in getting her own shoes on. They've worked hard to attain their competence. Let them know you think they're the greatest.

Teaching Kids To Make Good Decisions

Learning to make good decisions, such as saying "No" to drugs or selecting appropriate friends, is one of the most important skills to teach our youngsters. And it's never too early to start.

Begin by giving your kids lots of chances to practice making decisions. Even the simplest choices--"Do you want to wear these pajamas or these tonight?"--teach children to evaluate options. As they grow older, they may ask assistance from the clerk in the toy store, or help choose their own wardrobes. Whatever the issue, provide many opportunities to make safe, age-appropriate choices.

Notice I said "age-appropriate." Don't let your seven year-old decide whether or not to go to school. And don't ask your pre-schooler if you should take the job promotion in another state. These are adult decisions. Instead, give them relevant choices, such as whether to join Cub Scouts or play soccer.

Support your kids' decision-making efforts. Let them know when they've made wise choices, no matter how insignificant the issues are. For instance, giving your toddler hearty praise when he makes a good choice in the supermarket -- "Justy, you picked the perfect number of bananas for our dessert tonight" -- subtly prepares him for his teen-age years, when he'll need to make decisions about parties and sex.

Teach children how to evaluate data in order to make informed choices. A discussion with your 15 year-old daughter might go like this: "Let's see, you have swimming practice until 5:30, and you said Mrs. Allen wants you to baby-sit at 7:00. You also mentioned a biology test you have to study for. I think you're right. You'll have to tell Mrs. Allen you can't take the job this time."

Praise youngsters who have made good decisions, no matter what the context. Sometimes your child may find himself in a bad situation--one he knows you'll disapprove of--but he makes the right decision while he's there. Always support his positive decision-making efforts first. Discuss the misbehavior later.

Here's what I mean: Your teen-age son borrowed the car without permission, then was involved in a minor traffic accident. He calls you from a local pay phone to report the incident and ask for your assistance in handling the crash. While you may be furious he took the car without asking, you still support his decision to call for help.

Never ridicule your child's poor decisions. Let's face it. We've all made them. Instead, empathize with the fact it's no fun to make errors. Then take the opportunity to help re-evaluate the situation and find a better way to handle it.

For instance, your tenth-grade daughter went out with her friends the night before her history mid-term and, as a result, did poorly on the exam. Rather than being angry at her for getting a bad grade, discuss what choices she made and how they affected her performance. Then, encourage her to explore options that will help her do better next time.

Boredom Has A Place In Children's Lives

Bored kids are many parents' nightmare. The folks perceive it's their responsibility to entertain their children. They may even feel guilty or inadequate if Junior doesn't have enough to keep him busy.

In fact, a little boredom plays a positive role in youngsters' development. It stimulates their own interests and imaginations. It elicits internal forms of diversion and amusement, rather than depending solely on outside sources.

Boredom fosters creativity. It allows kids to combine the resources at hand with the ideas in their minds to recreate their worlds in whatever manner they choose.

Today they may be Eskimos and tomorrow they may be astronauts--all without leaving their yards.

Unfortunately, parents often stifle this creativity by bombarding their children with too many things to do.

Lots of toys and parent-orchestrated activities keep tots entertained. But the result is dependence on external factors for amusement, and a lessening of the ability to entertain themselves.

Television is one of the worst culprits. Psychologist John Rosemond, author of *John Rosemond's Six-Point Plan for Raising Happy, Healthy Children,* writes: "Television-watching inhibits the development of initiative, curiosity, resourcefulness, creativity and motivation."

He adds, "Television-watching interferes significantly with the development of a long attention span."

Since pre-school youngsters watch an average of four hours of TV per day, it's little wonder their abilities to amuse themselves are seriously impaired.

Dr. Rosemond explains, "Today's children are bored precisely because parents provide them with so many things and activities."

He goes on to say, "Instead of providing children with ample opportunities and the raw materials with which to find and create handmade playthings, we overdose them with mass-produced toys that stimulate relatively little imaginative thought--toys that are nothing more than what the labels on their boxes say they are."

Don't get me wrong. Dr. Rosemond and I aren't advocating an environment devoid of all stimulation and toys. We don't want parents to psychologically abandon their youngsters under the guise of promoting creativity.

We're simply stating that activities done *to* children hinder activities coming *from* the children themselves. By cutting back on the numbers of toys and outside resources, kids will be more successful at developing their inner capabilities.

The solution lies in letting go of the myth that our kids' lives must be three-ring circuses. We are not responsible for keeping them perpetually entertained. It's OK--even necessary--for them to think, "I'm bored. What can I do now?"

Provide your children with several age-appropriate toys and activities and plenty of space for them to be outdoors. Then allow them to do what they need to do most--play. If your child returns to you for amusement, direct her back to her toys. It's fine to play with her periodically throughout the day. But avoid allowing her to rely on you as her playfriend.

Whatever you do, resist the temptation to turn on the television for her. If she knows that's an option, she's less likely to ever play well by herself.

Kids And Money
It's Never Too Early to Develop Sound Financial Habits

Teaching kids how to manage their finances is as important as teaching them chemistry or math. But many parents take the old savings-in-the-sock-under-the-mattress approach and assume their youngsters will somehow learn about money on their own.

The goal isn't to create little Rupert Murdochs. Rather, it's to teach boys and girls wise saving and spending habits.

<u>Start early</u>. Even very young children can learn the value and importance of saving money. Small weekly allowances or payments for helping with chores can be tucked away for safe keeping until a special excursion to the toy store or market.

<u>Teach spending strategies</u>. Talk with young children about wise use of their money. They'll naturally want to buy the first toy they see, then the second and the third. Discuss with them what they would really like to play with, or what toy might last the longest.

<u>Support wise spending decisions</u>. Let children know when they've shown good judgment with their money: "Ryan, you got three gold fish for the price of a more expensive fish. That's what I call good value."

<u>Encourage saving</u>. Help your kids get into the "spend a little, save a little" habit. Perhaps you have them save 50% of their allowance and keep the other half free for spur-of-the-moment fun.

You might even match their savings dollar for dollar. If they save $5, you add another $5 to their savings account.

Help them avoid getting side-tracked. Most children change their minds about what they want as often as they change TV channels. Today they're clamoring for a hamster, tomorrow they have to buy a skateboard.

One solution is to write down all desired items on separate slips of paper, then put each one in a jar or shoe box. When youngsters earn enough money to make a purchase, they can look through the box to see what they want. Of course, interests will have changed and they won't even want some of the toys. But they'll be able to determine which items had long-term value. This technique also helps defuse the "I-want-it-now" blues.

Pay kids what their worth. If you pay your youngsters for baby-sitting or other chores, it's important to pay them the going rate. For example, don't pay your third-grader $2 for mowing the lawn when you'd pay a gardener $15 for doing the same job. This doesn't mean you pay them union scale. But you do want them to develop an accurate sense of their economic value.

Teach good buying skills. Several years ago my son, then seven, wanted to buy a walk-man. During the time he was saving up the money, we visited several different electronics stores and let him look over the various models. He told the clerks what price range he could afford and what features he wanted. He then tried out all of the options. The process required lots of time and patience, but he eventually made an informed decision and bought exactly what he wanted.

<u>Set realistic savings goals</u>. Help kids decide on reachable financial goals. My sons often dream about buying used fighter jets when used wet suits are more within their scope.

<u>Keep motivation high</u>. Children can get easily discouraged when they can't buy what they want NOW, so it's important to keep their energies focused and their spirits high. Help them make a chart showing how much they need to earn and how much progress they've already made. Some stores will lay an item away, allowing the child to pay in installments. You can also buy small portions of the full item, for example buying bird food one time, bird toys another, and finally the cage and canary.

Talking To Your Children About Sex

Uh-oh. Junior's just asked the dreaded question, "Mom, where do babies come from?"

Many parents live in fear of discussing sex with their children. They pray a few mumbled facts about the birds and the bees will suffice their youngsters' growing curiosities.

What most moms and dads don't realize is that sex education goes beyond one anxious talk in the library. Rather, it's a daily process that begins as soon as an infant is born. Parental attitudes about elimination, nudity, and babies' normal explorations of their own bodies are readily absorbed as children develop.

For example, a mother who slaps her baby's hand when he reaches for his genitals is giving him a negative message about his body and sexuality. On the other hand, a parent who helps his child learn socially appropriate times and places for self-exploration passes along a more positive message about sex.

Parents themselves constantly model sexual behavior. Whenever they kiss, hug, hold hands or flirt with one another, they are giving their children lessons about how to be loving, sexual adults.

Even so, talking about sex with your kids can be tricky.

Start by preparing yourself for the inevitable questions. Buy a good book about reproduction when your child is very small and keep it around the house to refer to with your youngster when the first questions crop up. You can even use a book about pregnancy or fetal development that you had on hand before the child was born.

Keep your answers simple. In fact, one or two sentences worth of information are usually all that are required. When your three year-old daughter asks why her brother has a penis and she doesn't, a simple response such as, "Because that's the way boys' bodies are made," may suffice. Avoid lengthy lectures on comparative anatomy.

Provide only the information asked for. It's easy to go overboard and give elaborate explanations when all the youngster wants is a direct answer. A pre-schooler wanting to know where babies come from doesn't necessarily want to hear about fallopian tubes or testicles.

If a child does want more information, give it. In fact, keep giving simple explanations until the youngster seems satisfied.

Always be truthful. Even a very young tot can be told honest facts. And don't be afraid to use the correct words. You don't necessarily have to use medical terminology. But slang and vulgar terms demean the very process you're trying to explain.

Speaking of vulgar slang, children usually start asking about such words when they reach school. The best approach is to explain the meaning of each word, then add, "But that's not a good word to say."

Take advantage of the opportunity to incorporate your moral values in your discussions with your child. Pepper your discussions with words about love, marriage, commitment and respect. For example, you may describe intercourse as "a loving act between a mommy and a daddy who care very much about each other."

The goal in talking to your child about sex is not only to impart information, but to encourage your child to come back with future questions. Therefore, keep the mood light, positive and loving. Avoid lecturing. And never laugh at or demean your youngster.

While I wholeheartedly encourage parents to talk to their children about sex, I realize that some are too embarrassed to do a good job. If you're in this situation, find someone who can help you. Your school's nurse, a teacher, a minister or family physician would all be good places to start.

Chapter 2

Discipline

"For the very true beginning of
her wisdom is the desire of discipline;
and the care of discipline is love."

The Apocrypha

10 Common Discipline Mistakes

I recently read an article entitled, "Ten Worst Discipline Mistakes Parents Make...And Alternatives," by James Windell, author of *Discipline: A Sourcebook of 50 Failsafe Techniques for Parents*. His material is worth repeating.

Mistake #1--Yelling. Yelling is for venting anger, not changing kids' behavior. Children of frequent yellers soon learn to tune out their parents' rantings. The result? Parents feel the need to yell even more to get a response from their youngsters, and kids feel hostile toward their folks. Try waiting until you're calmer to talk with your child, then make a firm, but reasonable, request or command. Save yelling for a real emergency, when you want your child's attention.

Mistake #2--Demanding Immediate Compliance. Commands to "Do it now!" show disrespect to the child, and are often ignored or tuned out. Instead, make a respectful request, then praise your child's prompt response. For instance, when your daughter puts her crayons away the first time you ask, give her a smile and say, "Thanks for doing just as I asked."

Mistake #3--Nagging. Mr. Windell believes that nagging is a problem for parents who try to be lenient or permissive. They don't want to get angry, but find themselves constantly reminding their children to comply. The parents feel resentful and angry, and the child still has not obeyed. A better solution? First, get the child's full attention, then state your expectation or request. Next, praise your youngster when your orders are carried out. If your child still fails to follow through, impose a negative consequence.

Mistake #4--Lecturing and Advice-Giving. Lecturing is futile. Not only do kids have a limited attention span for being "talked at," but lecturing seldom finds a solution for the problem at hand. For example, lecturing your child about rude behavior does little about teaching him a more appropriate way to behave. Advice is still necessary. Just give it in smaller doses, and make use of informal opportunities to teach a lesson.

Mistake #5--Taking Anger Out On Kids. Overreaction and inappropriate anger are common results of our high-stress society. You can tell when you're overreacting if a similar incident in the past didn't provoke the same response in you. The result is that kids feel confused and hurt by your actions. If you do overreact, don't be afraid to share a heartfelt apology. You'll be saying to your child, "Hey, we all make mistakes." And you'll be providing a time to share feelings and infallibilities.

Mistake #6--Shaming and Belittling. Sometimes we don't realize how our words hurt our youngsters. Statements such as, "Quit acting like such a baby," "That was so stupid," or "You never were very smart," cause kids to feel inadequate and insecure. Check your words before you speak. Ask yourself how you would feel if a boss or spouse spoke to you in the same way.

Mistake #7--Setting Traps. Mr. Windell notes that parents who tend to be punitive and authoritarian sometimes try to catch their children in a lie to prove a point. He cites the example of finding a friend's note in your child's room that mentions smoking. A trap-setter asks, "Do you or your friends smoke? No? Then what about this note?" Your child is put on the defensive, and learns to lie and mistrust his parents. Instead, use straightforward inquiry: "I found this note in your room that concerns me. Can you help clear this up for me?"

Mistake #8--Imposing Excessive Guilt. Some parents imply that their children are responsible for the circumstances of their parents' lives. Statements such as, "Look at all I've done for you, and this is how you treat me?" cause the child to blame himself for the problems of the world. Instead, handle your own problems yourself, seeking professional help if needed.

Mistake #9--Physical Punishment. The purpose of discipline--to teach your child self-control--is never accomplished through physical force. Children feel hostile and resentful, and the behavior is seldom prevented from occurring again. Seek developmental information on teen and child behaviors, and attend one of the excellent parenting classes offered in the community.

Mistake #10--Coercion. Using physical force to get the child to do what you want is most likely an example of your need to control the child's behavior. The child ends up resisting, and a power struggle ensues. Instead, give the child a choice: "Do you want to hold my hand going into the doctor's office, or do you want to go in by yourself?" This offers the child some power, but leaves no doubt about the expected behavior.

Constructive Alternatives To Punishment

There's one word I'd like to remove from parents' vocabularies--punishment. According to Webster, to punish means: 1) to cause a person to undergo pain, loss, or suffering for a crime or wrongdoing; 2) to impose a penalty on a criminal or wrongdoer for an offense; and 3) to treat in a harsh or greedy manner. If our goal as parents is to teach and guide our children into appropriate behavior, then punishment has no role in the process.

When punishment is used on children, it tends to set up an adversarial relationship between the parent and the child. It creates an atmosphere of "us against them." Kids come to view Mom and Dad as the enemy, and often go to great lengths to get even for what they perceive as unjust treatment.

Instead, parents and their youngsters should optimally see themselves as a team with the mutual goal of helping the kids grow into responsible and competent adults. Ideally, we should be able to convey the message, "I'm on your side," rather than, "I'm out to get you."

This does *not* mean that kids and parents are equal members of the family, or that children can do what they please. Parents must maintain full authority of the family. They must also expect top standards of comportment from their kids. Clear guidelines for acceptable behavior should be established, and, when youngsters stray outside of those guidelines, they should be quickly brought back into control.

But instead of using punishment, I prefer parents to use behavioral "realignment" with their children. Just as in the practice of chiropractic, where the goal is to keep the vertebrae in line without damaging the spine, so parents can realign their youngers' actions without resorting to more drastic, sometimes destructive measures.

A realignment is nothing more than an action you take to change your child's behavior. It simply states: "What you are doing is not OK. You need to stop, and you may need to experience a consequence as a result of what you have done." The purpose of a realignment is to guide a child back into the boundaries of acceptable behavior, and never to inflict any physical or emotional pain.

To distinguish between a punishment and a realignment, ask yourself the following questions:

Is this action I'm taking toward my child **RESPECTFUL** of that child. Punishment usually aims to belittle or demean the person being punished, while the goal of realignment is to respectfully correct behavior.

Is this action I'm taking toward my child **RELATED** to what the child has done? Mopping up the spilled orange juice is related to the child's act of rough-housing at the breakfast table. Spanking the child is not.

Is this action I'm taking toward my child **REASONABLE?** Not allowing a fifth-grader to ride his bike for the weekend because he forgot to wear his helmet to school is reasonable. Grounding the same child for a month is not.

Is this appropriate action being done **RAPIDLY**? The longer you wait, the less impact your response has. Do it quickly, then move on to something else.

Let me give you an example. Last year, one of our sons was having trouble completing school assignments. His work was habitually late, incomplete or sloppily done. We decided that whenever an assignment was not turned in on time, he would have to miss the next event in his life, whether it was a scout meeting, a tennis lesson or playtime with a friend. His schoolwork miraculously improved, and he never had to skip any of the fun.

If you find you are regularly feeling the need to resort to punishment with your children, I recommend you attend one of the many excellent parenting classes offered in your area. This will help you develop the skills you need to create more harmony at home.

Clear Parenting
Know What You Want Before You Ask It

One common mistake parents make with their children is not being clear about what they want them to do. These moms and dads have never decided how they want their youngsters to behave.

The result is that parents give their kids vague commands to "Behave," "Do better in school," or "Be more responsible." But they've never told them exactly *how* they should do it. Both parents and children end up frustrated and confused, and little behavioral learning takes place.

Fortunately, this problem can be easily solved with a technique I call Clear Parenting.

Clear Parenting means deciding specifically what you want your children to do *before* asking them to do it.

Here's how it works. Let's say you want your son to clean up his room. Normally, you'd tell him, "Hey, this place is a mess. Get it cleaned up." After he'd reported it was clean, you'd point out, "But you forgot to pick up your clothes. And you still need to clear off those shelves."

With Clear Parenting you select three to five specific tasks you want completed in order for his room to be considered clean. (Any more than five is usually confusing to both you and your child.)

In this case, you determine that you want him to:
1) Make his bed

2) Put away all clothes, either in the hamper or the closet

3) Clear off his desk

Next, express those tasks to him in a way you can determine whether or not they've been done. I call these "yes-no" statements.

"No shoes on the floor" is a "yes-no" statement. You can definitely assess if it's been finished.

"Get this stuff out of here" is not a "yes-no" statement. You can't tell when that command has been completed.

When your son has finished with the three directives, he's done cleaning his room. If he hasn't, he stays until he's done.

The benefits of Clear Parenting are many. It minimizes confusion, chaos and anxiety in the house.

Clear Parenting provides straightforward guidelines for your youngsters. They know exactly what is expected of them and how to go about meeting those expectations.

You are less apt to feel taken advantage of by your children. You're more aware about how you want things to run, and in less anguish when there are problems.

I recently used this technique with my nine year-old son. He wanted to sleep in several different locations in our house. At first I let him do it, since our boys often sleep on the floor in their sleeping bags in the playroom or in front of the fireplace.

But I began to grow resentful. He was leaving bedding strewn everywhere. And I was growing tired of the mess.

This time, instead of getting crabby and dramatically kicking blankets out of my way whenever I encountered one of his "nests," I asked myself, "What do I need to happen here? Where is the problem, and what has to happen to fix it?"

The answer was clear to me. He needed to pick up all the blankets, pillows and stuffed toys throughout the house, and to start sleeping in his own bed.

Of course, he protested at first. But I was clear about what actions I wanted, and he quickly complied. Had I been less clear, I have no doubt that he would have been more resistant.

Clear Parenting does not imply that we must parent like five star generals. It does not, in any way, imply a lack of compassion or nurturing of our kids.

In fact, quite the opposite is true. There's nothing more loving than providing our children with clear directives for their behavior. They'll spend more time mastering their life skills, and less time interpreting what their parents want them to do.

Pre-Praising Your Children
Setting the Stage for Positive Behavior

Did you know it's smart to praise your children for good things they haven't even done yet?

Pre-praising youngsters for characteristics and behaviors you want to instill in them furthers the development of those same qualities, and increases the likelihood they'll be manifested often.

Pre-praising requires three phases. The first phase, Setting the Stage, involves establishing the expectations you have for your children. You assume from them characteristics you want them to develop. Rather than waiting for them to show you they posses them, you tell them that they already do.

For example, you tell your daughter on the first day of kindergarten that you know she is a capable girl and will have a great time in school. Or you remind your children as you enter a restaurant that they are well-mannered and can behave appropriately during dinner.

You're not waiting for them to show you a behavior. You're telling them ahead of time you know how well they will behave.

Wise teachers use this technique often. My son's third grade teacher has the words "We Are Thinkers" prominently displayed in the classroom. Another teacher may assume the class motto "Room 3 Does Super Work!" A high school teacher may proclaim "The Class of '95 Reaches for the Stars!"

The second phase, Proving the Point, offers support for children's efforts in developing the desired qualities. For instance, if you have pre-praised your child for being trustworthy, you point out instances when he behaves in a trustworthy, responsible way. You may point out that he returned the lunch money he borrowed the previous day. Or you may mention he remembered to bring you a note from his teacher.

Your observations don't have to be earth shattering. Instead, they are simple statements that he is behaving in the manner you have expected.

The final stage, Finding Solutions, is for when children are *not* behaving in the expected manner. In these instances, you still pre-praise them for the behavior you expect, then help them discover alternative solutions that fit within the desired framework.

Here's what I mean. You have been pre-praising nine year-old Tommy for being honest. Then, you realize he has taken money from your wallet without asking. Rather than berating him for being a dishonest crook, you still tell him he is honest. But you make it clear that he is never to get into your wallet without permission. Next, you explore with him other, more appropriate ways to handle his desire to buy something.

You might say, "Tommy, I know you're an honest guy, but my purse is off-limits to you. How else can you earn money for those baseball cards?"

Pre-praising works because it presents a high standard of behavior in a very palatable way. Kids usually tune out our lectures and naggings. But pre-praising builds an atmosphere of cooperation.

Pre-praising helps kids view themselves positively. They feel they are already competent and valuable, then gear their behaviors accordingly.

Pre-praising supports youngsters in their daily efforts to develop strong characters. Let's face it. It's not always easy to tell the truth, resist taking drugs or behave responsibly. Recognizing their gradual steps toward mastery lets them know we appreciate their strides.

Pre-praising doesn't consider mistakes to be failures, but rather as opportunities to learn new solutions.

Finally, pre-praising helps parents see their youngsters in a new light. Rather than focusing their attentions on their children's flaws, they come to see their kids as the competent young people they are capable of being.

Praise
A Powerful Parenting Tool

Praise is one of the most powerful tools in a parent's arsenal of discipline techniques. Unfortunately, it is often misunderstood.

Simply put, praise is the display of approval for a child's behavior.

It may be verbal--"I like the way you didn't interrupt." It may be non-verbal, such as smiling and patting your toddler on the back as he sits quietly on your lap in church. It can even be written: for example, a note from your son's teacher commending him on his cooperation with his classmates.

Some people disagree with the use of praise. They feel it's unnecessary to praise youngsters for behaviors they should automatically be doing. Such folks feel silly or phony praising kids for accomplishing mundane tasks. They may even feel it spoils a youngster by telling her she's done a good job.

However, research and practical experience show praise offers many benefits to both parents and their kids.

First, it lets children know they've done what we wanted them to do. Too often, we give a directive--"Get along with your friends"--without ever saying when they've completed what we asked.

"Don't hit," "Quit fighting," or "Stop yelling," tell youngsters we don't like what they're doing. Only statements such as, "You've been sharing your toys this afternoon. I like that," give them direct feedback on their performances.

Praising their efforts--"You've studied hard tonight. I know your history grade is going to come up"--offers encouragement and motivation.

Praise also gets parents thinking about the good things their children are doing. Sometimes parents operate from the "No-Stop-and-Don't" point of view. The result is usually critical parenting, followed by resistance from the kids.

If, on the other hand, we team up with our kids, explaining what we want, then praising them often when they meet our standards, we create an atmosphere of cooperation and goodwill among family members.

Here's an example:

Several months ago, my first-grade son, Neil, received a note called a "Super" from his school, commending him for picking up trash on the playground. Know what he's been doing daily ever since? That's right...picking up trash during recess.

A few last pointers on praise:

* Praise often. You can't have too much of a good thing.

* Praise effort over outcome. Don't wait until your tot has mastered tying her shoelaces. Praise her effort and determination along the way.

* Be sincere and subtle. A quiet nod, a gentle pat, a thumb's up sign or a whispered, "Way to go!" are as effective as backflips when it comes to praise.

Learning to Say "No" To your Youngsters

I've adopted a new parenting persona: Attila the Mom.

I'm a conqueror of the "whining gimmes," a gladiator in the "war against more." I'm untiring, unbending and relentless. And I'm convinced my kids are better off for it.

I started out as Mrs. GreatHeart, unending provider of childen's needs. "You want that? Let me get it for you. You want three more just like it? I'll give you those, too."

I fulfilled kids' needs non-stop. But my children were never satisfied. And I was perennially pooped.

No matter how much I gave them, they always wanted more. They expected gum every time we passed through the check-out counter. After one toy, they wanted two.

They never reported having enough love, affection, food, toys, time with friends, vacation...You get the message. The only things they had in excess were chores and homework. No matter how much time, energy, effort or cash were expended on them, they always had one more request.

That's when I wised up. I realized they were caught up in the *process* of wanting, rather than experiencing actual needs. No matter how much they were given, their quests for more would continue.

The one thing they really needed was a sane mother who could help them put a lid on their endless "gimmes." They needed someone who didn't wait until she was a basket case before saying that final "No!"

Psychologist John Rosemond agrees with me. In his book, *John Rosemond's Six Points for Raising Happy, Healthy Children,* he writes about the importance of giving youngsters a healthy dose of Vitamin N--his term for saying "No."

His advice to parents: "Stop thinking that your first obligation is to make and keep them happy, because it is not. Your first obligation is to endow them with the skills they will need to successfully pursue happiness on their own."

Giving in to their every whim only prepares them to expect others to do the same, a dangerous and unfair message to send our kids.

Children certainly do have basic needs we must provide for them. Food, medical care, clothing, shelter, safety, comfort, education and a few playthings are minimal requirements for insuring our youngsters' survival. But few of our kids are lacking these basics.

My boys have stacks of toys in their playroom, endless choices of healthy food in our kitchen, two devoted and nurturing parents and a loving home environment. Deprivation is definitely not an issue.

Instead, the issue is setting limits and sticking by them. I now snuff out the first, "Mom, can we buy...?" at the grocery store. I release guilt when they beg me to take them somewhere. I turn deaf ears on the whines accompanying every departure from friends' houses.

I don't even try to explain myself, rationalize my decision or plead for their cooperation. That only tends to heighten their feelings of self-pity.

Lest you wonder, I'm basically a nice person. And I think the world of my two kids. But let me hear one "whining gimme," and I turn into Attila the Mom.

Enlist Your Youngsters' Help In Solving Problems

Enlisting your children's help in finding solutions for their own problems is an effective learning and problem-solving tool.

For example, Maryanne enlisted Brian's help in working out a schedule for doing his homework. She asked, "Brian, let's figure out when is the best time for you to do your school work. Is it after school? Before dinner? Or before bedtime?" Together they discussed the pros and cons of each option, then selected the one they thought best.

Enlisting youngsters' help teaches them good problem-solving skills. They learn to critically analyze their own situations, then devise workable solutions.

It encourages them to take responsibility for their own problems. No longer can they blame Mom or Dad for making poor decisions for them. Rather, they gain power over their personal lives, and must live with the consequences of their choices.

Children are more cooperative when they feel invested in their decisions. Because they help select options that fit their personal habits and schedules, they are more likely to follow through on their self-structured plans.

Enlisting children's help minimizes parent-child power struggles. Parents are removed from the role of "bad guys" who forever make demands of their kids. Rather, they are blended into a partnership with their youngsters for the purpose of devising mutually agreeable solutions.

Finally, enlisting children's help in solving their own problems takes a lot of responsibility off of parents. They no longer have to guess about what will work with their sons and daughters. Instead, they ask their kids to share the burdens of solving appropriate problems.

Of course, not all issues are subject to discussion. Sherry shouldn't enlist her children's help when deciding whether or not she should remarry. And Frank and Jeanne shouldn't enlist five year-old Reuben's help in deciding if he should wear glasses. Some decisions must be made by the adults.

However, within the framework of an already made decision, there may be room for opinions: "Girls, Rob and I have decided to get married. I'd love your help in planning the wedding."

Even very young children can help make their own decisions. When Louise had a brief appointment, she asked five year-old Ryan, "Ryan, you're going to need to sit quietly in the waiting room while I talk to someone at my office. What do you want to take with you so you won't be bored?"

How can you go about enlisting your children's help? First off, define the problem. Are your kids arguing over phone privileges? Are they chronically late for school? Do you need to take a long trip in the car? Be as specific as possible, and stick to one issue at a time.

Next, brainstorm all the possible solutions.

Let's say you're trying to decide which child gets to sit in the front seat. Think of all the ways you could handle that problem: 1) The first child to the car sits in the front. 2) The child who claims the front seat first can sit there. 3) One child sits in the front seat going to the location; another sits in the front going from the location. 4) All children sit in the back seat.

Pick the most agreeable solution. There may need to be some bargaining: "I'll sit in the back seat, but he can't listen to only his radio stations." But choose the one best fitting everyone's needs.

Evaluate your solution after a specified length of time. Has it solved the problem? Does it need some refinements? Should you start over and try something different?

I recently used this technique with my two sons, ages twelve and nine. A neighbor had granted them permission to cut through a gate in her yard on the way to school. But soon every young boy in the neighborhood was using her pathway. After brainstorming numerous options, our boys suggested putting a lock on the gate with a combination only our two families knew. This solution not only solved our dilemma, but reinforced valuable problem-solving skills.

Don't Fall Prey To Childish Antics

Sometimes parents resort to the same, inappropriate behaviors as their youngsters. They hit, bite, name-call and even throw tantrums. From a distance it can be hard to tell who's the child and who's the adult.

It starts when parents forget their innate positions of leadership and feel they must compete with their kids for control. For instance, when five year-old Wylie calls his mother "Dummy," she defensively responds by saying, "Hey, you're the dumb one around here." Or, when twelve year-old Jay smacks his unsuspecting father on the head with a snow ball, Dad picks up an even bigger chunk of ice to throw back, yelling, "Maybe this will teach you a lesson!"

What these parents fail to realize is that such negative behaviors are wrong no matter who does them. Becoming ensnared in a youngster's childish actions not only fails to improve the situation, but usually makes it worse.

Let me give you an example. Elisha, six, grabbed a cookie from her mother's hand, protesting, "Hey, that's the last one and it's mine." Mother, stunned, grabbed it back and scolded, "Don't grab things, you little brat. You need to learn to share." Elisha then hit her mother, crying, "Give me my cookie! Give me my cookie!" Mother, in desperation, spanked her daughter on the bottom, and yelled, "Don't hit me! You're not getting anything to eat. Go to your room!"

Who was acting childish? Of course, Elisha was being immature when she demanded a cookie, grabbed it from her mother and then hit her to get it back. But her mother exhibited the same inappropriate behaviors of grabbing, hitting and being demanding. She was threatened by her daughter's outburst and felt she needed to restore control over her child. However, she did nothing to minimize her daughter's frustrations, nor to teach Elisha better ways of handling the situation.

What would have happened if Mother had behaved more like an adult? Perhaps, when Elisha grabbed the cookie, Mother could have said, "Wait a minute, Honey. Please don't grab from me. Tell me what you want and we'll see what we can do about it." Then, when Elisha stated her desires, Mother could have said, "How can you ask me politely for this cookie?" Mother would have been helping her daughter learn good manners, sound problem-solving skills and great techniques for lowering frustrations.

What can you do if you notice you're being as childish as your tot? First off, take five. Back away. Separate yourself from the game of "one-upmanship," and regain your composure.

Recognize your children's tactics. What are they doing that is inappropriate? Pinching? Cheating? Sticking out their tongues? All kids try these antics sooner or later. It doesn't mean they're evil or that you're doing a rotten job of raising them. Instead, they're displaying normal childish behavior. It's your job to teach them other, more suitable, ways of acting.

Stay in authority. Don't get into a power struggle. Know that you're the parent, and act accordingly.

Decide what behavior you'd prefer. Not saying, "I hate you?" Not kicking his sister? Not hitting you with her magic wand? Be clear about what you want from your child, then calmly explain your desires.

For example, if four year-old Julie keeps bumping the baby's stroller against your legs while you attempt to talk to a friend on the sidewalk, say, "Julie, please stop bumping into me." If she persists, patiently take her hand, explain again what you expect, then make sure that she complies.

Don't become ensnared by the childish demands. Rather than scolding a tantruming toddler, for instance, calmly escort him to his bedroom and tell him, "When you have calmed down, I will be happy to see you out in the living room." Or instead of lecturing your eighth-grader for her selfish behavior, simply state, "Kate, I've said 'No' and I don't want to hear any more about it." Then walk from the room to avoid further protests.

Chapter 3

Strong Families

"A life is beautiful and ideal only when we have taken into our consideration the social as well as the family relationships."

Havelock Ellis
1859-1939

Characteristics Of Strong Families

In honor of November being National Family Month, I would like to share with you some of the factors that make families strong.

About ten years ago, two researchers in Nebraska, John DeFrain and Nick Stinnett, founded a project that studied more than 3,000 families in the U.S. and around the world. Through questionnaires and interviews, they were able to determine six characteristics common to all successfully functioning families.

These traits were consistent in spite of variations in the families' racial backgrounds, levels of education, income, religious persuasions and ages. They applied to two-parent as well as single-parent homes.

What are the characteristics of a strong family?

<u>Commitment</u>. Members of strong families value their union. They are dedicated to each other's welfare and happiness. Members report such sentiments as, "My wife and kids are the most important part of my life," and "Divorce is not an option for us."

Everyday problems don't diminish the commitment felt by the members of strong families. They feel a pull to stay together, in spite of life's ups and downs.

<u>Appreciation</u>. "The expression of appreciation permeates the relationships of strong families," note the researchers. Rather than taking each other for granted, these family members go out of their way to make each

other feel special, loved and capable. The outcome is that self-esteem is boosted, and family members thrive.

<u>Communication</u>. Strong families have good communication skills and spend lots of time talking together. Members report making time to keep up on each others' lives. Husbands and wives may plan a quiet evening out or families may gather around the dinner table. Wherever the locale, strong families keep the pathways open for ideas and sharing to flow.

<u>Time Together</u>. As a family counselor, I've learned one of the best indicators of a family's mental health is the amount of time members spend together. Members of strong families are no different. They regularly mention the importance of gathering together for holidays, working together on chores, sharing meals, taking vacations together and chatting together at the end of the day.

While one of the realities of modern life is that we all have activities and demands constantly tugging at our sleeves, strong families have learned not to lose sight of their primary purpose: to keep their families functioning and healthy.

<u>Spiritual Wellness</u>. Whether or not they are involved in a formal religion, strong families are aware of a greater good or power in their lives. It may assume many titles: belief in God, faith in humankind, concern for others or strong ethics. But the outcome is the same. Members of strong families experience a unifying force, a caring for one another, that transcends each individual's needs. They are committed to the well-being of an entity greater than each member. And that

entity--the family--is something not to be undone by the whim or fancy of one person.

<u>Coping Skills</u>. Strong families are able to turn crises and turmoil into opportunities for growth. They don't have *less* stresses in their lives. But they are able to keep them from destroying their lives. They may use such coping skills as problem-solving, getting outside help or relying on spiritual resources. Whatever the method, strong families have developed their skills and support systems to enable them to weather life's traumas.

Keep in mind that these are characteristics of *strong* families, not *perfect* families. All families struggle with daily pressures and life-threatening crises. What is exceptional, however, is that strong families are surviving families. By utilizing these traits, they not only overcome their tribulations, but grow stronger as a result.

Special Moments
The Gems of our Families' Lives

Special moments--we all remember them. They're the times we spent with that special someone, free from hassles or distractions, completely focused on what we were doing. Perhaps we were going through a picture album with Grandma, or helping Mother bake a cake. Maybe we helped Uncle Don fix our bicycle, or sat fishing with Dad by the lake. Wherever we were, or whatever we did, the moment is now permanently etched in our minds, providing us with feelings of love, safety and serenity whenever we recall it.

Special moments play important roles in our lives. For example, they create bonds between family members and friends. Participants share their secret memories for years after the event.

Special moments provide opportunities to talk. Little else is interfering, so they're a great chance to get to know others.

Special moments connect generations. Since some of our most cherished memories can be those shared with elderly relatives whom we knew only as young children, those memories bind us to family members who lived in previous times. Family lore and history can be handed down as we listen to Great-Grandpa tell his tales.

Special moments also cement family relationships to withstand the not-so-pleasant times every family must endure.

Special moments seldom happen during life's Big Events. Weddings, trips to Disneyland and Thanksgiving are usually fraught with tension, distractions and high expectations. Of course, these events play an important role in the lives of families. But they're less likely to be the settings for the special moments we cherish into adulthood.

Instead, special moments happen in quiet, uncluttered times. Husking corn on the back step, folding laundry or watching rain hitting against the windows are settings when special moments might occur.

While you can't make special moments happen, you can create an atmosphere that fosters their occurrence. Allow plenty of unhurried time with your children, grandchildren or other relatives and friends.

Avoid over scheduling relatives' visits. Instead, set aside chunks of quiet time. Use simple activities, such as working puzzles or shelling peas, to bring people together and provide opportunities to chat.

Don't be afraid of boredom. Special moments often result when two people seek something to do.

We may not always be aware when special moments have occurred. What may seem uneventful to an adult may leave a lasting impression on a child. And, what may pass undetected by a youngster may be monumental to her grandmother. The common thread lies in the fact that, however insignificant the event feels at the time, its memory is cherished for years to come.

Family Dinners
A Great Way to Build Family Relationships

The family dinner, once the mainstay of the American evening, has unfortunately gone the way of the poodle skirt and the rumble seat. These days, if you ask who's coming to dinner, the answer may too often be, "No one."

Why bother with family dinners? Lots of reasons. Family dinners provide structure and continuity to days that can be downright crazy.

Family dinners give families time to be together. Studies have shown that the average parents spend a mere eight to 11 minutes a day with their children. Add the 20 minutes it takes to eat dinner, and you've substantially increased time with your kids.

Family dinners allow members to catch up on each others' lives. They can hear about band practice, hockey try-outs or playground friendships.

Family dinners are good times to solve problems. Together you can discuss savings strategies for the next vacation or decide the best time for Sis to practice her French horn.

Family dinners can be great opportunities for you to discuss values. Not only can you impart your ideas on the big issues, like drugs and birth control, but you can listen to where your children stand on these dilemmas.

Finally, family dinners let your kids practice their table manners. While manners shouldn't be the focus of the mealtime, they can be taught and reinforced on a daily basis.

One high school in Missouri feels so strongly about the importance of family dinners that its students' parents must sign an agreement stating they'll eat dinner as a family five nights a week. Explains the school director, "It seems like such a basic kind of thing, but it does work. Kids today need a certain basic structure, and if they don't have that structure, they don't know where they are. They just thrash around until they find some limits."

I can already hear the protests: "With work schedules, Camp Fire and dance lessons, there's no way we can all sit down together." But, with dedication, persistence and creativity, you can include family dinners in your home.

Start by making them a priority. Enlist your spouse's help. Solicit older children's cooperation. If there's dissention in the ranks, explain the importance of sharing time together.

Find one night that fits everyone's schedules. Don't expect miracles. Just start small to get everyone used to the new regime. And don't demand perfection. The goal is simply realistic conversation, not a seen from a Norman Rockwell painting.

Keep expectations to a minimum. Remember, you're just eating together, not convening to write the Constitution. You needn't discuss world politics or the meaning of life. Being available to each other is enough.

Avoid making this a gripe session. Instead, keep the tone pleasant and enriching for everyone. An occasional mention of manners is fine, but don't spend the whole time harping.

Can't for the life of you find a common evening? Then how about sharing breakfasts before work and school? Or spending time for a leisurely brunch on Saturday mornings?

If you can't find *any* time during the week, then re-evaluate your priorities. After all, family dinners are not only nutritionally satisfying, but they nurture healthy relationships as well.

Assuming Leadership In Your Home

Today's parents have ceded family leadership to their kids. The coup has been a subtle one. But the result is that many moms and dads are unwilling or unable to take control of their children.

The reasons are numerous and complex. Divorced and blended families often give youngsters garbled signals about who is in the driver's seat. As more and more children cope with the challenges of split and re-structured homes, a larger percentage of youngsters are unsure of where they stand.

For example, Janine, a newly separated mom, told her ten year-old, Derrick, that he was now the man of the house. While it may seem appropriate to Janine to turn to her child for support, that action elevates Derrick to a role he is not ready to assume, and accords him the same authority as an adult.

In another situation, Mark and Diane want to marry and combine their children from previous marriages into one household. Yet, when disputes erupt, both adults express stronger allegiance to their own children than to each other. Such ambiguous alliances inhibit the establishment of clear leadership in their new family.

Duel-career households or single-parent families can be required to expend so much energy at their jobs that they are too tired to adequately oversee their children. Some youngsters adapt well to this situation, and develop into responsible and self-sufficient boys and girls. Others, however, flounder without proper guidance and fall prey to drugs, anti-social behavior and gangs.

Faulty leadership is a problem for other families. Some parents have become paranoid about making mistakes with their youngsters, or somehow hurting their children's feelings. These parents don't stick with decisions, are easily swayed by their sons' and daughters' protests and accept blame whenever problems arise. Sure, we all want to raise our kids as best we can. But defensive parenting is not only ineffective, it also lets children know the adults aren't really in control.

What can you do to re-establish authority in your family? Start by recognizing you've given up control, and make a priority to regain it.

Establish clear guidelines for your children to follow. Don't cave in, no matter how hard they protest or whine, "All the other kids can do this."

Strengthen your marital relationship. A solid adult team provides good leadership, and has more resources to devote to problems. Take plenty of time to be together without children.

If you are a single parent, hold your ground. Don't let the kids undermine your authority. I know it can be exhausting. But make clear decisions and muster the courage to stick with them. Whenever possible, enlist the help of other adults, perhaps an uncle or sister, to back up your policies.

Blended families, work hard at cementing your marital relationships. Family loyalties can pull you in many directions, so try to present a unified front. Make your own rules for your home; don't fall prey to the phrases, "But we can do that at Dad's house," or "You're not my real mommy."

Set priorities for your time. Cut out all extra demands so you can focus on your kids and family responsibilities.

Get support from your school and community. Talk to your children's teachers, school counselors and youth leaders for moral support and back-up. Don't feel you are alone. You have lots of people who can help you.

Finally, take good care of yourself. Parenting can be a real challenge. Nobody deserves a break more than you do.

Nurturing Spirituality In Your Family

The arrival of young children spurs many couples to rekindle their interest in attending church. Whether it's to help Junior answer his question, "Daddy, where do we go when we die?" or a response to the pressures from well-meaning parents and in-laws to raise the grandchildren in the faith, new moms and dads often find themselves feeling it's time to bring religion into their lives.

Lots of parents are active in churches before their kids are born. They either practice the religion they were raised in, or have found another that better meets their spiritual needs.

But others let religion lapse while they're in school, dating and starting careers. They find God to be less relevant than the want ads, a new condo or a great weekend.

That all changes with children. Parents, concerned about the moral development of their youngsters, flock to the pews Sunday morning. Moms volunteer to teach Sunday School. Dads serve on finance committees or act as Elders.

Of course, there's nothing inherently wrong with the "Let's-Do-It-For-The-Kids" converts. Certainly, any exposure children have to spiritual training is worthwhile.

What these well-meaning folks are overlooking, however, is that spirituality is more than weekly church attendance. It's not something you can give your kids, like a DPT vaccination. Rather, spirituality is a lifestyle devoted to religious principles, a commitment to thoughts and beliefs that are evident in every aspect of your life. Going to church or temple without those convictions is like only brushing your teeth before visiting the dentist: you don't feel good about doing it, and it's certainly not very effective.

What can you do to establish religion as a central part of your life? Start by analyzing your spiritual needs and preferences. Think about your beliefs and decide how best they can be expressed. Question what you hope you and your family will gain by attending church.

You may allow previous religious training to guide your decision. Or you may choose to let go of childhood teachings in favor of new messages that are more relevant to your current way of thinking. Recognize there are no hard and fast answers. Only you know what will work best for you and your youngsters.

Visit a number of different churches to see which feel right. You may try out several of the same denomination or a variety of different religious approaches. No one will be perfect. Instead, look for a philosophy you agree with and an atmosphere that welcomes you back.

If you and your spouse are of different religious upbringings, it's still possible to reach a workable solution. You can discuss which of you is most convicted about your spiritual principles, then allow that person to make the choice. You can combine the symbolism and lore of both religions, to create a rich fabric of multi-culturalism. Or perhaps you choose a new, joint faith, unencumbered by previous backgrounds.

Whatever you do, make a final decision. Don't attempt to practice two conflicting religions simultaneously. I've known children who attended temple one week, and mass the next. But such kids rarely feel convicted to either philosophy.

Always attend services with your children. Never expect a child to attend a church you don't also attend. One well-meaning mother told me how she used to drop her daughter off at Sunday School, then go back to bed for another hour before returning to pick her up. Such an approach teaches kids little except confusion and hypocrisy.

Finally, make your family's spiritual expression a joyous, celebratory time. Through the principles of charity, hope and love that are inherent in all religions, you'll be drawing your family closer together while providing members with important tools for improving their daily lives.

Let Your Children Know You Love Them

Do our children know we love them? Often times they don't. Between discipline, disappointments, lost tempers, expectations and high levels of stress, the message of how we really feel toward our kids can get lost.

Let me give you an example. Denyse, 15, was brought into my office by her parents. She sat slumped in her chair, her stringy, jet black hair nearly covering the sullen expression on her otherwise attractive face.

"She's completely changed," bemoaned her mother. "She has stopped going to school, hangs around with the wrong crowd and is totally uncooperative around the house."

After listening to every family member complain about this child, I asked her parents, "Why are you so concerned about her behavior?"

"We're afraid she'll ruin her life," they replied.

"And why are you so worried she'll ruin her life?" I again probed.

Her parents hesitated. "Because we love her," they finally stammered. "We don't want anything to happen to her."

Denyse's parents *did* love her. But the only messages she was hearing were anger, disappointment, frustration and hopelessness.

Children need to feel loved by their parents. When they don't, they feel rejected, isolated and unlovable.

Their self-esteems plummet. They may feel pressure to prove their worth to family members and friends. They may seek out activities and groups who make them feel lovable. Or they may simply give up, rationalizing, "If my own parents think I'm worthless, no one else will like me, either."

How can we make sure our kids feel loved? Start by telling them often. I'm convinced you can't say, "I love you," enough. Tell them to their face, let them overhear you talking to a relative, leave them a note...Any way you do it, let them know you think they're terrific.

I know, sometimes they don't act very lovable. And they're lucky we don't put them on the next bus out of town. But those are the exact times when we need to most clearly convey our feelings. It's easy to love our children in the good times. It's imperative that we love them in the bad.

Let's say your seven year-old son has been sent home from a friend's house for fighting. You're tempted to lecture him about his behavior and ground him for the rest of the afternoon. But this time you realize he needs your support, not your rebuke. You gently put your arm around him and profess, "Hey, Buddy, I love you more than anything else in the world. Let's figure out what the problem is with you and Tim."

I'm not advocating that parents become pushovers, or that they abdicate their authority in the name of showing how much they love their youngsters. Sometimes the most loving actions parents can take is to say "No," or to hold fast to their convictions. The key is to convey those sentiments within the context of love, rather than anger, frustration or a desire to punish the child.

Here's what I mean. Your pre-teen son has broken a window during a wrestling match with his pals. You are angry because you already told them to go outside if they were going to be rough. But he's very apologetic, and he's mortified you'll blow your stack. You're tempted to simply take care of it, knowing how scared he already is. But you also want him to be responsible for his actions. You tell him, "I love you, and I know this was an accident. Let's work out an arrangement where you can earn part of the replacement cost of the window."

But what do you do when you blow it? When you don't show any love for your child, and instead hurl insults, accusations and threats?

First off, try to catch yourself before you say the wrong things. Tell your child, "I'm too upset to talk about this right now. I'll come back after I've cooled down."

If you've already spouted off, don't panic. We've all done it. Simply wait until you're more settled, and apologize to your child. "I'm really sorry, Rebecca. I completely lost my temper. I said some rotten things, and I apologize. I love you so much, and our relationship is important to me. Can we go back to square one and see if we can do better?"

There's No "Right Way" To Raise Children

Mona approached me recently at a meeting: "Linda, I want to do the best possible job of raising my children," she sincerely stated. "But sometimes I feel guilty because I'm not sure I'm doing it right."

Mona is obviously a caring parent who wants nothing but the best for her youngsters. But what Mona, and many well-meaning parents like her, fails to realize, is that there is no one, correct way to raise children. There are as many possible methods as their are parents and kids.

Since humans have inhabited this planet, children have grown up under vastly different circumstances. For the most part, each culture has done a commendable job of creating youngsters who are able to survive the rigors imposed by their lives.

Just as each country operates under its own set of laws and ethics, so each family is a unique system requiring its own policies and practices. Such factors as a family's religious beliefs, their economic status, the parents' professions, the numbers and ages of their children, their ethnic heritage and their personal lifestyles and philosophies all contribute to the shaping of parental policies.

Rather than anxiously searching for the "right way," parents should trust their own instincts and ask themselves, "What works best for us?   What child-rearing methods can we implement that fit our individual styles?"

How do you go about this task? Start by gathering as much information about parenting as you can. Read books. Take classes. Attend workshops at your church or at your youngster's school. Talk with pediatricians, teachers, pre-school directors and experienced parents. Become acquainted with the latest methods and philosophies. Absorb as much as you can.

Next, filter this information through your own personal belief system. Decide which ideas you and your spouse agree with. Discard policies that don't feel right to you. Analyze which methods will work in your family. Remember, just because an expert says something, doesn't mean your family has to do it.

Finally, implement the methods you think are best for you and your kids. They may not be trendy or popular. But parents shouldn't feel they must conduct Gallup polls of their friends and neighbors every time they make decisions for their families.

For example, when Pamela was pregnant, she read lots of books about breastfeeding. She took a class at her hospital, read literature from her doctor's office and talked to friends who urged her to nurse her infant. But when Pamela's son, Dennis, was born, she found that breastfeeding was not something she enjoyed. It wasn't that she couldn't do it; she just felt constricted and uncomfortable with the act of nursing. Pamela knew breastfeeding was good for little Dennis, but she also realized that her peace of mind was as important as her child's source of nourishment. She, therefore, opted to bottlefeed her child.

In another instance, Tom and Francie decided they didn't want their daughter, Hailey, to date until she was sixteen. They knew this policy would seem strict to other kids and parents at Hailey's high school. But their personal and religious convictions guided them away from allowing earlier dating.

When developing your own parenting policies, follow these three "R's":

1) **Be respectful** to both you and your child. Avoid hitting, shouting, name-calling and all other forms of belittlement or personal insult.

2) **Be reasonable**. This is open for interpretation. But grounding your daughter for a week for riding her bike through your new flower beds is unreasonable. Having her spend an afternoon helping you replant your seedlings is more appropriate.

3) **Get results**. If your methods work, use them. If they don't, try something else. When it comes to your family, you're the leader. Don't be afraid to take charge.

Family Celebrations
Build Bonds and Boost Self-Esteem

Want to strengthen your family's relationships, increase your children's motivation and have a lot of fun? Great! Celebrate with your kids.

Family celebrations are events that acknowledge members' accomplishments or important moments. They may recognize an academic or physical achievement, or note passages of life. They may cheer family financial successes, or applaud emotional or psychological victories.

Celebrations are more than just fun. They instill positive behaviors or values. They convey to your children what's important to you, and reward their energies in those areas.

For instance, if you celebrate your son Raymond's improved reading grade, you're demonstrating that you value your children's education.

Celebrations reward kids' motivation. They acknowledge their hard work and diligent efforts, and show your approval of those characteristics.

Celebrations give support to family member's individual progress. They say, "We're with you all the way," an important sentiment to convey to our youngsters.

One family I know celebrated the father's lowered cholesterol levels. Another, applauded their daughter's efforts in her speech therapy.

Celebrations give each child a chance to be recognized. This can be especially important when one child is overshadowed by siblings who are older, more capable or more aggressive.

Celebrations boost family members' self-esteems. Public acknowledgment for their everyday triumphs helps them gain feelings of competence and importance.

Celebrations involve all members of the family in everybody's lives. For instance, if the children live with their mother during the week, but visit Dad on the weekends, he can celebrate in their week's successes, even though he wasn't there when they happened.

Finally, celebrations pull families together. They create an atmosphere of joy and camaraderie for all members, and establish an upbeat tone for the whole household.

What can you celebrate? Anything! Nothing is too small or insignificant. A newly loosened tooth, an improved spelling grade, a more cooperative attitude...Any positive event can be grounds for family accolades.

I once awarded one of my children a certificate of merit because he had become more helpful around the house. Another time we staged a family celebration because we'd paid off a second mortgage on our home.

Don't wait for straight A's or making All-Stars before breaking out the proverbial champagne or Seven-Up. Kids who are already successful in school and sports don't need as many boosts as the ones who are struggling with their math facts or lagging behind in their coordination.

That doesn't mean you don't applaud those top achievers' efforts. Of course you do. Just remember to applaud *all* children's successes with equal fervor, no matter how seemingly inconsequential.

When it comes to celebrating with your family, the sky's your only limit. You might make a favorite meal, dine at a fancy restaurant or splurge at the local yogurt shop. You may choose to write a letter, send a special note, draw a picture or create a congratulatory banner. How about composing a commemorative song or delivering a standing ovation when the celebrity enters the room? You can even use the simple, but highly effective, three cheers, "Hip-hip-hooray! Hip-hip-hooray! Hip-hip-hooray!"

However you do it, make your celebrations simple and festive. Don't go overboard and put pressure on yourself. After all, you're not staging a bar mitzvah. Instead, enlist all family members' help, creativity and energies. This is one case where homespun and heartfelt are definitely best.

Expectations For Your Youngsters
Keep Them Realistic

Don played college football ten years ago and always dreamed of coaching his own son. But his wife recently delivered their third child--another girl--and he's having a hard time dealing with his disappointment.

We all have expectations for our children. We fantasize this daughter will be the first member of the family to graduate from college, or this son will set a world record.

Unfortunately, many parents fail to realize that babies are born with their own unique agendas. Their goals are not to fulfill our personal longings, or meet our emotional needs. Rather, they are to define and realize their own inner potentials, regardless of how they blend with ours.

For instance, the child we planned to be an athlete may prefer reading to running the track. The daughter we steered toward the opera may dream instead of raising goats for 4-H. And that youngster we vowed would be the next President of the United States may instead be born with Downs Syndrome.

Of course, this doesn't mean we can't encourage our kids to join us in our favorite pastimes. Certainly exposing them to our interests increases the likelihood theirs will be the same.

But developing similar interests and living up to our expectations can be vastly different. For one thing, our expectations are seldom--if ever--met. If the child does go into athletics, is making the team going to be enough? Or must the child win trophies and compete at the regional or state levels?

Expectations usually involve a great deal of pressure. Kids are no longer pursuing an activity because they like it, but rather because of parental demands. Should the children at some point lose interest, they must bear their moms' and dads' disappointments, and risk being perceived as failures.

What can you do if you have unrealistic expectations for your youngsters?

Start by recognizing them at work. Ask yourself, "Is this my child's interest, or am I expecting her to fulfill my dream?"

Give up your preconceived notion of who your child will be. I recently heard a deaf comedian explain how she helps people cope with their grief at having a physically challenged child. She encourages the parents to build a tiny coffin and fill it with descriptions of the perfect child they had expected to have. The couple then buries the image, and turns its focus to the real child in their family.

Tune into your child's strengths. Make a list of what your youngster does best. Include everything, inter-personal as well as physical and academic talents. Then replace any supposed short-comings with those positive attributes. For example, your daughter may never be tops in her class, but she may have a smile that brightens the whole room.

Find common interests you share with your youngster. If you can't find any, create some. Perhaps your son isn't as interested in art as you are, but the two of you love to build model airplanes.

Finally, just because your child doesn't fulfill your dream, doesn't mean you can't still pursue it. You might choose to coach a local sports team or found a neighborhood youth program. The important thing is to take responsibility for meeting your personal needs, not misdirect them onto your child.

Titles Of Respect
The Importance of Calling Adults "Mr." and "Mrs."

Many parents allow their children to address adults by their first names. But what appears to be a harmless trend toward familiarity may actually be heading families for trouble.

Titles of respect have traditionally been used in our culture to differentiate relative social or professional status. People with higher status, such as advanced age, education or authority, were given titles reflecting their positions. Referring to someone as Doctor, Monsignor, Captain and Mr. and Mrs., inferred respect for that person's place in life.

Calling people by their first names, on the other hand, implies that the speaker is on an equal or higher status than the person being addressed.

Americans are uncomfortable with this system of acknowledged status. We want to think of ourselves as equals, that no one holds greater importance than another.

But, of course, this isn't true. We *do* have different levels of education, knowledge, experience and authority. A surgeon performing an operation *does* have specific knowledge and skills. The pilot guiding the airplane in which I am traveling *does* have training and experience. My sons' principals *do* have authority over their respective schools.

When children call adults by their first names, they are unconsciously implying they are of the same status as those adults. The youngsters' language suggests they have similar rights and privileges as mature members of our society. Their words denote a lack of respect for the adults whom they're addressing.

This is where the problems come in. Children do *not* possess the same status as adults. They do *not* have equal rights or privileges. And they *do* need to feel and demonstrate respect for adults.

This is not to say that children should not be cherished, nurtured, loved and respected. Of course, they should and must be. They are our greatest treasures.

But they are young, immature people. They are not ready to be adults. They don't want the responsibilities that accompany adulthood. They, therefore, should not address adults as if they were on equal footing. Their language should refer to adults as "Mr." and "Mrs." And their tone should reflect the appropriate respect.

When children fail to address adults as "Mr." and "Mrs.," they are less likely to feel the need to comply with the adult's wishes. After all, to their way of thinking, adults and children are equals. No one has authority over the other.

On the other hand, when children address adults respectfully, they are more apt to behave respectfully. There is less likelihood of disobedience, back talk or rebellion.

I must make a confession. Being called Mrs. Griffith was difficult for me at first. The name sounded too formal, and seemed way too old for a woman as young as I perceived myself to be. Besides, the name had already been claimed by several other women in my family, namely my mother- and grandmother-in-law.

But I changed my tune when I recognized the importance of teaching my children to be respectful. I didn't want my boys viewing themselves as equals with every adult they met. Sure, I wanted them to feel confident and secure. But I also wanted them to realize children have different rules than adults. I wanted them to be clear that adults--not children--were the leaders.

Of course, terms of address aren't the only indicators of respect. Some youngsters can say "Mr. Smith" all day, and still be rude and out of control. And other boys and girls can be less formal with adults, and be wonderfully polite and cooperative.

There's also room for interpretation. Relatives should use their family title, such as "Aunt Meggie" or "Grandpa Hal." Special family friends may earn a loving term of endearment, as in "Mr. B" or "Miss Carol."

There may even be special circumstances where adults wish their last names to remain anonymous, for example when a spouse is a police officer or when a last name is too cumbersome to be easily pronounced. In such instances, grown-ups may opt for a nickname or simply use their first names.

Overall, however, it's important to establish consistent standards of respect that transfer across language, attitude and behavior.

Humor

A Treasure to Share with Your Loved Ones

The gift I'd give to all families? The gift of humor. I'd love to see Mom and Dad sharing a chuckle, parents giggling with their children and kids belly laughing with each other.

Growing up has become too serious. Parents feel burdened by responsibility and guilt. They spend millions of dollars on books telling them how to raise competent and intelligent youngsters. Yet they approach the task of rearing their offspring as if they were attending a funeral.

Kids feel pressured, too. They must not only master the three R's, but say "No!" to drugs, avoid sexually transmitted diseases and dodge bullets on the campus. It seems being young has become more of a prison sentence than a phase of life.

I know life isn't a bed of roses, and sometimes we just don't feel like laughing. But the times when life is most dismal are actually the times we need humor the most.

In fact, life wouldn't seem so oppressive if families would let themselves laugh more. Parents, enjoy your children. Allow yourselves to revel in their honesty, innocence and youth.

Don't die of embarrassment when your toddler puts her finger in her nose while you're showing her to the relatives. All toddlers do it. Chortle at her delightful lack of self-consciousness, then give her a big, warm hug.

And don't tear your hair out when your son and all his friends gallumph through the house leaving every door open in their wake. Set some guidelines for their behavior. Then laugh at their boyish energy, and send them back outside.

Even the normally serious task of discipline can be done in a light-hearted manner. Let me show you what I mean:

Your daughter's room looks like a landfill, and you've been after her for weeks to clean it up. But this time, rather than lecturing, you add humor when asking, "Hey, is this your bedroom or an archeological dig? I'll give you until dinner to uncover the ruins." She may still not pass white glove inspection, but you will have assumed a lighter attitude.

One morning, I snapped at my two sons for wrestling in the kitchen. As I stood nearby, watching them stare morosely into their cereal bowls, I proclaimed loudly, "Boy, Mom sure is crabby this morning." They burst into laughter. They had gotten the message that the kitchen wasn't a playground; there was no sense in their continuing to feel miserable .

Keep in mind the Golden Rule of humor: a joke or statement has to be funny to everyone involved. If someone isn't laughing, then their feelings need to be respected, and that topic kept off limits.

Never laugh *at* a child. A youngster's mistakes or lack of knowledge may indeed seem humorous to adults. But the damage ill-timed laughter can cause to tiny egos is never worth the few moments of grown-up hilarity.

Recognize the difference between humor and sarcasm. Humor's intent is to entertain. Sarcasm has the underlying purpose of making someone feel bad.

To check whether your attempted humor is, in fact, sarcasm, ask yourself honestly, "Do I want this person to be hurt by these words?" If the answer is in any way, "Yes," then avoid making your remark. It's never OK to rationalize your sarcasm with the words, "It's just a joke."

Because much of humor is learned, you can build your kids' humor quotients by telling jokes around the dinner table, reading funny books together and renting comic videos. You may have to help them understand why something is funny, but you'll be giving them the gift of humor in the process.

Sibling Camaraderie
Helping Children Build Bonds Between Themselves

Sibling camaraderie is the sense of love, caring, respect and shared history brothers and sisters feel for each other. Families that value sibling camaraderie not only help their children develop strong, lifelong relationships, but also create a more harmonious atmosphere at home.

To nurture sibling camaraderie, start by paying less attention to sibling rivalry. Sure, sibling rivalry is a nuisance. But it plays a vital role in helping kids develop their interpersonal skills. You can probably ignore 90% of your children's bickerings. Instead, encourage them to get along and work out their own solutions.

Teach your children constructive problem-solving techniques. Help them develop strategies for sharing their toys with each other, deciding whose turn it is to sit in the front seat of the car or who does which household chores.

For example, you might help your daughters negotiate who gets to speak on the phone at which times during the night. Perhaps they can make out a schedule so each girl has specific times she can make calls, and they can establish a policy for handling in-coming calls and controlling the length of their conversations.

Establish a "get-along" attitude in your home. Expect members to be respectful and considerate of each other. When inevitable problems arise, express your faith in their abilities to handle situations, then allow them to work them out.

Discourage name-calling and rude language among siblings. Let your kids know vulgarity or calling each other names, such as "Idiot," "Ugly," or "Moron," is not acceptable. Explain that disrespectful phrases, such as "Shut up," and "Get lost," hurt feelings and create a negative atmosphere. You're not expecting your kids to be perfect. But you are sending a clear message that they need to get along in your household.

Model respectful behavior for your children. Youngsters learn what they live; when mom and dad are caring and considerate of each other, they provide the best and earliest lessons for their kids to follow.

Praise cooperative behavior among your children. If your pre-schooler shares half of her sandwich with her younger brother, give her a big hug and comment, "What a caring sister you are. Tony's one lucky little brother!"

Avoid competition among siblings. Minimize the times they go head-to-head, where only one child can be the winner. Instead, look for opportunities where all children can be successful, or where the whole family works as a team.

For instance, rather than seeing who can clean his room the fastest, have children see how quickly they can all clean up their rooms.

Look for cooperative activities that foster positive family relationships. Family outings, camping trips and projects pull siblings together and create strong bonds.

Never compare your children's grades, athleticism, physical appearances or popularity. This can be especially debilitating when one sibling is less talented than another. Rather, value each child for his or her uniqueness, recognizing accomplishments on many different levels.

In one family, Craig was a gifted student, while his sister, Janet, struggled in her high school classes. But rather than focusing on Janet's lower grades, her parents supported her successes in drama.

Sibling camaraderie doesn't develop overnight. Rather, it is an ongoing process of learning and maturation. With patience and perseverance, parents can give their children one of life's greatest treasures-- strong relationships with their brothers and sisters.

Birth Order Helps Define Who We Are

Is your only child a perfectionist?

Is your oldest child bossy?

Is your middle child a good negotiator?

Is your youngest child charming?

Then you and your children are experiencing the effects of birth order, a profound influence in all of our lives.

Simply put, birth order is the position we occupy in our family as we grow up. Each place tends to describe certain characteristics about our upbringing: i.e. an only child has no siblings; a youngest child is the last one born in the family.

Of course, birth order does not say anything about other influential factors, such as our family's financial status, or if our parents were divorced. But people with certain birth orders have been shown to share some personality features.

According to Lucille Forer, Ph.D., in her book, *The Birth Order Factor*, first-born and only children tend to be higher achievers than other children in the same family.

"Because of their close relationships with their parents," she writes, "these youngsters commonly develop high verbal ability." Such kids generally succeed in school, score well on intelligence tests and set lofty standards for themselves.

Dr. Forer notes that, of the first 23 American astronauts, 21 were only children or first-borns.

Unlike only children, however, "first-borns are often jealous or anxious as a result of being superseded in the family nest," she says. They may also feel dissatisfied with themselves due to excessively high expectations placed on them by first-time parents.

Middle children are more difficult to categorize because of the numerous family constellations that can make up the "middle" position. In general, though, Dr. Forer describes second-born and middle children as being diplomatic because they are forced to work around older, stronger siblings. They may be friendlier and more adaptable than first-borns. They tend to have an easier time with their parents.

On the other hand, second-born and middle children don't seem to do as well in school as their older brothers and sisters. In fact, they may have more problems in school due to aggressiveness and competitiveness, possibly brought on by the need to prove themselves to others.

Youngest children are the family babies, according to Dr. Forer, and often remain that way throughout their lives. They may receive special privileges from doting relatives, or, in large families, they may be ignored by over burdened parents. Last-borns tend to be playful and light-hearted, but they may also become dependent on others to make decisions and take action for them.

What can you do about the effects of birth order? Begin by recognizing how they color your perception of your world. For example, if you're an oldest child and you've felt an unending need to succeed, you may be able to correlate it to a desire to please your parents.

Releasing yourself from the internal struggle frees your energies for more realistic, constructive pursuits.

Provide children with opportunities to assume roles different from their birth orders. For instance, try not to have your youngest child also be the youngest member of his grade. Or give an only child lots of chances to interact with other kids. You'll be encouraging new experiences for your youngsters, while broadening their range of social skills.

Chapter 4

•

How We Talk To Our Children... And How Our Children Talk To Us

"The music that can deepest reach, And cure all ill, is cordial speech."

Ralph Waldo Emerson
1803-1882

Improving Your Family's Communication

The words "communication" and "common" originate from the same Latin root word, "communis," meaning "shared by all or many." When we communicate with members of our families, we are literally imparting or sharing our thoughts and feelings with each other.

Those thoughts and feelings must travel freely along a roadway established between the communicating parties. Person A shares while Person B listens, then Person B shares while Person A listens. Communication is generally considered successful when that roadway has been kept clear so lots of information can be shared by both parties.

Communication breaks down when the roadway is blocked. One member of the party feels threatened or no longer wants to continue the conversation. A barrier goes up. No further sharing can take place.

Often parents inadvertently create roadblocks when talking with their children. Such common parental practices as name-calling, humiliating, yelling or passing judgment cause kids to clam up, tune their folks out and ignore them. Youngsters are saying, in effect, "I will not share with you if you are going to make me feel powerless and bad."

The goal, then, is to learn communication techniques that increase the likelihood of continued sharing.

Begin by using "I" statements when talking with your youngsters. Statements such as, "I need some quiet time," or "I was worried when I didn't hear from you," convey your needs and feelings without attacking anyone. "You" statements, such as, "You never help out," are aggressive in nature, and usually elicit an angry or hostile response.

Avoid losing your temper. When anger flares, communication changes dramatically. You're no longer sharing information, but rather trying to retaliate and hurt the other party. Damaging things are said and done.

It's imperative to stay calm. If you are too angry to talk about something, wait. Take a breather. Tell your kids, "I'm just steaming right now. I'll come back and talk to you later."

Listen--really listen--to what your child is telling you. Don't attempt to communicate while you're reading the newspaper or watching television. That simply tells a youngster you're not interested in what is being said.

Make an attempt to understand what your son or daughter is telling you. This doesn't mean you have to agree with it. But do try to understand it. Perhaps you can remember back to the same age and share a similar emotion or event.

Clarify what both you and your child are saying. "I'm not sure, but it sounds like you were embarrassed by what happened at school. Is that how you felt?" Your child can either agree with your assessment, or help you understand it even further.

Avoid making judgments. Remember, you want to keep the roadway open. Telling your son you hate his friends, or reminding your daughter she looks ridiculous are going to create immediate roadblocks.

Attempt some degree of resolution to the issue. This doesn't mean you solve your kids' problems. Or that every conversation needs to end with big smiles. Telling your teen he has lost the privilege of driving the car because he has been driving in an irresponsible manner is not going to please your son. But the message can still be conveyed with respect, and mutual sharing and understanding.

Lecturing
A Miserable--and Ineffective--Way to Discipline Children

Lectures are long scoldings given to children with the hopes of changing their behavior. They're torturous for the kids. And they're not effective for the parents.

Lecturing starts when moms and dads feel powerless about something their kids have done. They lecture in an attempt to regain control. Unfortunately, youngsters react to parental lectures with hostility and withdrawal. Parents end up feeling more powerless than ever, and resort to longer lectures.

Lecturing is similar to nagging, where parents repeatedly tell children to do something with little or no results. The difference is in the role assumed by the adults. Lecturing parents are seeking control over their kids. Nagging parents are pleading for their cooperation.

Why doesn't lecturing work? First, it fails to send a clear message to children about what their parents want. If Dad lectures his son about his poor grades, his disrespectful attitude at home, his sloppy room and his long hair, the boy still doesn't know what specific behavior his father wants him to change.

Second, lecturing puts children down. Since parents are trying to regain control, their lectures often belittle or ridicule their youngsters. Phrases such as, "You inconsiderate slob. You never think of anyone but yourself," not only make kids feel bad, but alienate them from their folks.

Finally, lecturing often results in a power struggle. Parents' efforts to gain the upper hand elicit needs for more control from their children. With each member of the family trying to outdo the other, there's little room for problem-solving or constructive communication.

Not sure if you're lecturing your kids? Ask yourself what you want when you talk with them. If you're trying to solve problems, share concerns or explain new family policies, then lecturing probably isn't involved.

However, if you're venting anger, attempting to dominate, proving you're right or pointing out someone's faults, lectures may be the result.

Fortunately, there's plenty you can do to break the lecture circuit. Start by deciding clearly how you want your child to behave, and stating only that message. For example, if you want your daughter to remember to bring her gym clothes home to launder, specifically convey those words. Don't lecture about the last time she forgot them, or the science project she didn't finish.

Don't overtalk. Keep your messages simple and straightforward. I like the approach taken by Jane Nelsen and Lynn Lott in their book, *Positive Discipline For Teens,* where they recommend parents restrict their communications to ten words or less. Say, "Please take out the recycling," rather than, "Isn't it about time you carried your weight around here? Do I have to do everything for you?"

Use "I" statements with your children. Stating what you need prevents you from lecturing them about what you think they need. Here's what I mean: Let's say your twelve year-old son is staying up too late, and you'd like him to go to bed earlier. Rather than saying, "You're being inconsiderate because you expect me to stay up so late waiting for you to get to bed," say, "I'm tired. I need you to get to sleep, please."

Identify the problem you're feeling powerless about and seek constructive answers. For instance, if you're feeling frustrated because your daughter's grades are slipping, don't lecture her about the importance of getting into a good college, or about how she's ruining her life. Instead, approach the subject rationally, and encourage joint solutions.

You might say, "Janey, I'm concerned about that last report card, and I was wondering if we could talk about it. Are there some ways that Dad and I could help you with your studying?" By passing on the lecture, you'll not only save her sagging self-esteem, but open the door for some good communication.

Rude Language Has No Place In Your Household

Rude language is more than bad words. It's a verbal assault launched against another person with the intent of gaining control over that person.

Rude language is an act of aggression that is only one step removed from physical violence. When children use rude words, they are actually attempting to psychologically intimidate or frighten other youngsters or adults.

Want proof rude language is aggressive? Just watch the reactions of those who hear it. First, they feel anger. Then, they respond with confrontation. If the rude words continue, fights usually ensue.

When family members speak rudely to each other, the results are equally destructive. Problems are seldom resolved because, when rude words are used, people stop looking for any workable solutions to their problems, and resort to threatening, bickering or fighting. Relationships are damaged, and family members' self-esteems plummet.

Unfortunately, rude language and behavior is on the rise. Schools report increasing numbers of verbal assaults against other students, teachers and school personnel. Television shows and movies portray more and more kids engaging in rude talk with adults and other youngsters. And more families are relating to each other in disrespectful ways.

What can you do to get rid of rude language in your household? Start by recognizing that rude language is a learned style of relating. Kids learn rude behaviors from their families, friends and the media. Those behaviors then turn into habits. Getting rid of rudeness means relearning new ways of relating to each other.

Let your kids know that rude language is *never* acceptable. Period. The goal of families is to develop and strengthen relationships among the members. If people feel they cannot relate to other members without responding rudely, then they must wait until they're calmer and can speak with more respect.

Mom and Dad, this goes for you, too. There is never an excuse for speaking rudely to your children or your spouse. Instead, use respectful, constructive means of communication. You'll be improving your marriage, as well as modeling better methods for the kids.

This doesn't mean we don't blow up sometimes. Of course, we all do. But loved ones are not our psychological punching bags. If we need to let it all out, we can jog, write a viscious letter we don't send, yell into a pillow, punch a real punching bag...anything but take it out on the family.

Don't let kids solve problems when they're mad, either. Always have them cool down before any negotiating begins.

Learn how to solve problems constructively, without put-downs or rude language. Whenever Rick and Diane used to argue, Rick would use rude words that would incite Diane to hurl back insults in retaliation. Now, they don't try to talk unless they're both calm. Then, they use "I" statements such as, "Rick, I have a problem with the fact that you want to be gone again this weekend."

Talk with your children about appropriate and inappropriate words. Explain the meanings of new, rude words they bring home from school, then let them know those are not acceptable words for them to say. Don't cave in to their pleas, "Everyone else can say that." Be firm, and set high standards for their behavior.

Never allow siblings to talk rudely to each other. Even the most innocent of rude comments can lead to hurt feelings and needs for getting even. It's best to avoid them altogether and teach kids other ways to relate.

Teach your children how to solve problems peacefully. Help little ones share toys with friends. Show older kids how to negotiate so each one can get what he wants. You'll not only be minimizing rudeness, you'll be giving them skills that will benefit them for the rest of their lives.

Name-Calling
A Detriment to Your Family's Well-Being

Name-calling takes place any time one person labels another in a way intended to put that person down or make him feel bad. It's a not-so-subtle form of verbal aggression. And it has no place in the family setting.

Name-calling can range from a toddler's silly "Dumb Head" to a teen's face-reddening obscenities. The common theme, however, is the intent to intimidate, humiliate or inflict mental anguish on the recipient.

While some names are always offensive, others are offensive only to certain people. For instance, calling a man who is 6'4" tall "Shorty" is not likely to be perceived as intimidation. Yet that same title, spoken to someone already self-conscious about his diminutive stature, can be construed as a hostile gesture.

Name-calling can also be specific to the intent of the speaker. Words uttered lovingly, for the purpose of conveying good feelings, are unlikely to be hurtful. Those same words, uttered in anger, or to put the recipient down, will feel like aggressive name-calling.

Here's what I mean. Four year-old Moses regularly burrows himself under his covers before his mom, Sue, tucks him into bed. When she gently calls out, "OK, you little wiggle worm. Time to come up for your kiss," her intent is to express loving feelings. She is not guilty of any name-calling.

On the other hand, when eight year-old Jessica is angry at her younger sister, she screams out, "I hate you, Sarah. You're an ugly worm-head. I wish you were dead." Jessica is verbally attacking her sibling. She is clearly guilty of name-calling.

Name-calling, at any level, is detrimental to positive family relationships. Since the primary goal of a family is to provide an atmosphere that is supportive and safe for all members, any form of intentional belittling is unacceptable.

Name-calling also lowers family members' self-esteem. Helena grew up with four older brothers who were allowed to mercilessly tease her and call her derogatory names. As a result, she never felt competent or worthwhile, and had trouble holding down jobs.

Not sure if you're guilty of name-calling? First, analyze your intent. If you discover you're subtly trying to intimidate, frighten or otherwise gain control of your youngsters, then name-calling may be the result. If, on the other hand, you honestly feel your purpose is to express warmth and positive feelings toward your children or loved ones, then name-calling probably isn't an issue.

You can also ask those around you if they feel insulted or belittled by your words. They'll be able to provide you with important feedback about how you're coming across to them.

Name-calling can even be a habit you're not aware of. For instance, James had never given any thought to the fact that he regularly called his young daughter "Dummy." His parents had said that to him when he was growing up, so he assumed it was acceptable to say to his child.

You can help stamp out name-calling in your family by establishing a "no name-calling" policy. Make all forms of name-calling off limits. Period.

If you or other family members are angry enough to want to call someone a name, take five until you're calmer and can use more constructive terminology.

Don't even let your toddlers call anyone apparently harmless names, like "Poopoo Face" or "Fat Head." Let them know early on that name-calling hurts people's feelings.

Patiently explain the meaning of each new inappropriate phrase your young child calls someone. Don't just say, "No name-calling, Peter." Instead, tell him, "It doesn't feel good to be called 'Fatso.' That's not a word we use."

Never tolerate name-calling by your teens. If they want to say something to you, insist they use polite, non-aggressive words. If they resort to name-calling, explain to them that you'll listen when they can speak to you civilly, then leave the room.

Finally, as a last result, institute a family-wide fining policy for anyone guilty of name-calling. The offender --parents included--must pay the recipient of the crime one dollar. You'll not only be helping wipe out name-calling, but you'll be playfully joining your kids in a worthwhile family cause.

Overtalking
Too Many Words, Too Little Listening

Overtalking is the use of too many words when speaking to children. It is usually done in an attempt to convince children to do something they don't want to do.

Overtalking often starts when parents believe that all youngsters, no matter how young, require lengthy explanations about everything happening in their lives.

For example, a toddler wants to crawl out of the shopping cart while his mother is shopping. An overtalking parent might tell the child, "Justy, standing up in the shopping cart is very dangerous. Every year, lots of little boys and girls just like you try to wiggle away while their parents are shopping. But the cart could slip out from underneath you, and you could go crashing to the floor and hurt yourself. That would be very serious."

A non-overtalking parent might simply say, "Justy, you need to stay seated, please. I don't want you to fall."

Parents who overtalk to their children feel out of control with their kids. They assume a pleading, begging role when they speak to them. Rather than telling their sons or daughters to comply with their requests, they feel they must convince them to obey. They keep adding more statements to their arguments, hoping their youngsters will take heed.

For instance, Lisa wants her five year-old daughter to turn off the television and go to bed. She firsts tells Courtney, "Honey, it's time for bed. I let you stay up an extra hour so you could watch your favorite show, so now it's your turn to do what Mommy asks."

When Courtney doesn't budge, she says, "Now Courtney, I never could stay up as late as I'm letting you stay up. And you promised me you would go to bed right after the show. You'll have time to watch television tomorrow. It's very late now, and children your age need plenty of sleep. You don't want to catch another cold."

On and on Lisa goes, trying to cajole her daughter into following her orders. Meanwhile, Courtney continues watching the TV.

Some parents resort to overtalking out of guilt or excessive concern to protect their children's self-esteem. They are uncomfortable making demands or setting limits on their youngsters. They feel extra words somehow soften the impact of their parental demands and restraints.

The results, however, are unclear parental messages. Kids never know what is expected of them. It's impossible for a child to decipher what's being said when his parent discusses his dirty room, lack of responsibility, lack of appreciation, poor study habits and lost library book all in the same paragraph.

Overtalking is similar to two other ineffective communication patterns--lecturing and nagging. All three involve excessive and futile talking by parents, and, in each case, kids fail to listen to what their folks are saying.

What can you do if you chronically overtalk to your kids? Start by giving them clear, short messages about what you want them to do. "You need to set the table now, please," tells your son exactly what you want him to do.

Be sure you have your kids' attention. Too often we try to explain things to them while they're watching television or playing with their friends, rather than waiting until they are fully focused on what we're saying.

Expect compliance from your youngsters the first time you give an order. Don't say something five times before you really want them to do it.

Be ready to back up a request. A statement such as, "You need to come in the house now," may require you to go out into the front yard to escort a reluctant toddler in.

Finally, problem-solve areas that aren't working. For example, enlist your family's help in figuring out ways for members to complete their chores without anyone needing to remind them.

Silencing Your Youngsters' Whining

Shannon Rose is a whiner. She whines when she's hungry or thirsty. She whines at the least little frustration. Sometimes she whines for no reason at all. She's driving her parents nuts, but they don't know how to stop her.

Whining is a high-pitched, irritating wail that almost all kids use at some time or another. It often happens when a child is exceedingly tired, stressed or over-stimulated. And, in those situations, it is usually stopped when the stressful events are eliminated, and the child is fresh and rested.

At other times, children whine because their needs haven't been met when they were expressed in a non-whining way. Youngsters end up feeling powerless over controlling their bodies or lives. They resort to whining in a desperate effort to be heard.

Let me give you an example. Five year-old Ginny is on a picnic with her parents and several families. Mom is sitting on a blanket with the baby, chatting with friends, and Dad is playing baseball. Ginny needs to be taken to the restroom. She approaches her mother, mentioning she has to go, but Mom brushes her aside, telling her she should have gone before they got to the park. Ginny goes to tell her father, but he's up to bat, and doesn't even notice she's at the field. Ginny, meanwhile, feels desperate and powerless over the situation. She returns to her mother, whining and crying. Mom angrily scolds Ginny for acting like a baby, then drags her off to the restroom.

This does not mean you must jump at every little want your children express. But it is important to let kids know you've heard their needs, then tell them clearly what you are willing to do about them.

Here's what I mean. Carrie, age seven, has just announced she is hungry. But you are talking on the phone long distance. Rather than ignoring Carrie until she is whining, you take a break from your call and address your child: "Carrie, you must wait for me to be off the phone. I will fix you a snack when I am done."

Let your children know whining is not an acceptable form of communication. You want them to use a grown-up voice to tell you what they want. If they have trouble using grown-up voices, you will help them know what they sound like. But you will no longer respond to whining.

Many younger children may not be able to verbally identify their needs, so you'll have to act as an interpreter. "Sounds like you're really frustrated with that toy, Collin. Let's put it away for now and read a book before naptime. Can you pick out one you'd like?"

When children are already whining, calmly tell them you hear them, but you will not respond until they have stopped whining. When they do use an acceptable tone, thank them for doing so, then respond to their needs: "That was much better, Cassy. Let's go get the juice you wanted."

If normally whiny children tell you something in a non-whiny voice, praise them for using a grown-up tone. "You know, Max, you didn't whine when you told me that. That was super! You're really using a grown-up voice now."

Should you have an event coming up that is likely to cause whining in your youngsters, let them know ahead of time you'd like them to cooperate without whining. Then look for possible solutions to help them minimize their whining. For example, if you are taking your children on a long car trip, and they often become restless and whiny, discuss with them the day before how you expect them to travel without whining. Then enlist their help:"What can you each bring to entertain yourselves while you are in the car?" You'll be teaching them appropriate behavior, then helping them take responsibility for how they act.

Breaking Kids' Interrupting Habits

Patty and Barbara meet on the street corner. They haven't been together in months, and are eager to catch up on each other's news. But Patty's six year-old daughter, Carly, keeps interrupting. While tugging incessantly on her mother's arm, she alternately whines that she is thirsty, that she's tired and that she's bored. Nothing Patty tries seems to work, so, after ten miserable minutes, the friends are forced to depart.

Learning not to interrupt is a difficult concept for all children. Because kids are innately self-centered, they have trouble waiting to get their needs met. In the case of interrupting, they may not even have a need until the parent's attention is turned toward someone else. Then, the child's primary need is to regain control of the parent.

As parents, our job is to help our youngsters delay their immediate wants while gradually becoming more aware of the wants of others in their world. We must teach them how to respect others' needs, yet still meet their own.

The process begins by first deciding you will not allow your child to interrupt you. Many parents think they can't have adult conversations with children around. This doesn't have to be the case. While babies may not be able to delay their gratification, a child of two or older is capable of being "put on hold" for a few minutes until you are ready to talk to him.

When he interrupts, explain that he will have to wait. Tell him, "You are interrupting. You must wait until I am done." This may have to be done several times during a conversation, but stick with it. Be firm. Let the child know he may *not* interrupt. Period.

Be sensitive to the appropriate length of time to make a child wait. With a very young child, under four years of age, finish your thought, then attend to his needs. A five or six year-old can wait five to ten minutes. An older child should be able to wait until your whole conversation is finished.

Of course, if a child has to go to the bathroom, is hurt or in danger, he requires immediate care. Put your conversation on the back burner until your little one is taken care of.

When you have finished your thought or conversation, or an appropriate amount of time has elapsed and you want to tend to your youngster, sincerely thank him for waiting. Let him know how much you appreciate his consideration. A statement such as, "I had a wonderful visit with Leslie because you were able to wait," makes him more likely to be patient the next time.

Be careful not to take advantage of your child. Don't expect your pre-schooler to wait 45 minutes while you talk to your accountant. And if you know he's going to have to be patient, you may want to help him out with a little toy or treat to entertain him while you talk.

Respect your child's needs not to be interrupted. Let him finish his explanations and stories without unreasonable interruptions. One of my sons pointed out to me several years ago that I was interrupting him too much. In general, show your children the same consideration you are hoping for them to show you.

These same guidelines apply whether you are talking to a person at the mall, on the phone or in your living room. It even holds true when you want a quiet moment by the fire with your spouse. Give a clear message: "Mommy and I want to talk by ourselves for awhile. You'll need to play until we are done." You'll be helping your youngsters gain self-control, and teaching them good lessons about respect.

Stop Nagging Your Kids

Nagging. Every parent hates it. We say the same things over and over, but children do little to comply with our demands. Threats, pleas, bargains and shouts fall on youngsters who no longer seem to comprehend the English language.

Parents feel angry and powerless. Kids feel badgered and demeaned. Frustration and animosity flourish, but the problems are never resolved, and no changes take place in our children's behavior.

What can you do to quit nagging? First off, listen to how you communicate with your children. If you repeatedly issue the same statement (for example, "Don't forget your lunch," or "Please quit running through the house!") but fail to get any results, it's time to try a new tactic.

Next, identify one problem area you'd specifically like to have your youngsters change. Notice I said just one, not twenty or thirty. Many parents attempt to change so many things at once, they overload and alienate their kids, and end up changing nothing.

Approach your children in a way that encourages communication. Kids who have been nagged tend to automatically tune out most of what their parents say, so it's important to approach them gently and constructively: "I'm concerned that you've lost your two best sweaters, and I know you miss having them to wear. Is there some way we can work together to make it easier for you to keep track of your clothes at school?"

Let them know you want to stop nagging them, and that you have a new plan. Explain how you'd like to make life more pleasant for all of you, but you need their cooperation. Avoid blaming or belittling. Instead, show them you're on their side.

Be persistent if they resist. For example, you might say, "I know you're angry at me because I have nagged you so much. But I'd really like to change how I talk to you, and I can't do it alone. I'm going to need your help."

Be specific about your expectations. Don't issue vague statements, such as, "Stop being so irresponsible!" Instead, decide on one or two precise actions you want to see happen; for example, "I want you to remember to feed the pets without my having to remind you every evening."

After deciding on what the problem is, take positive steps to solve it. Let's say your son regularly forgets his lunch, no matter how many times you remind him. Rather than nagging him every morning (which obviously is not working), enlist his help in coming up with a solution. Brainstorm together. Perhaps he can pack it in his backpack after breakfast, or he can put it by the door so he will see it as he leaves. He may even decide to buy his lunch instead of carrying it. Don't discourage creativity. But do encourage him to assume responsibility for remembering his lunch.

Back up your plan with consequences. For instance, if your son still forgets his lunch, then he goes hungry until dinner. If your daughter forgets to pick up her dirty clothes and put them in the hamper, then she goes without clean clothes, or she launders them herself.

Be open to negotiation. Perhaps your children will devise a plan whereby they clean their rooms thoroughly one day a week in exchange for your not nagging them to clean their rooms every night. Or maybe you agree to allow loud music to be played before 6:00 p.m., but not after dinner or before bedtime.

Avoid nagging your children out of habit. Unfortunately, the only way some parents relate to their kids is with nagging. If the youngsters changed all their folks complained about, these parents would still find new issues to nag for.

Instead, choose one issue to work with, then make a conscious effort to look for areas you can praise and support in your child.

Kicking Kids'
Bad-Word Habits

Bad words. Every child tries to say them, and every parent hates to hear them.

But whether you're dealing with a five year-old's overuse of "potty" words, an older child's attempts at hard-core expletives or any youngster's poor choice of phrases, the parents' goal is the same: to teach children appropriate language.

It's inevitable we have this problem. No matter how carefully we speak to our children at home, their environments are full of oral pollutants. Movies and television blare unusable language. Well-meaning relatives may say words we disapprove of. The schoolground is teeming with unmentionable phrases.

Since there is no right or wrong way to speak, each household must decide on its own levels of acceptability. Social, ethnic and religious backgrounds all play a role in determining patterns of language.

How can you best handle your child's bad words?

Start by making sure you don't use any words or phrases you don't want your children to say. They learn how and what to say by listening to their folks. If you don't want the kids to say it to Grandma, then you'd better not say it to them.

Most of the time, very young children don't understand the meanings of what they're saying. They're simply repeating what they've heard from someone else.

Provide them with simple definitions, then explain, "Those aren't good words to say."

Discuss definitions with older children, too. Talking about the facts of life and bodily functions in scientific terms helps demystify the words, clarify the biological processes, and makes your youngsters less likely to depend on their buddies as sources of information.

It's guaranteed that at some time your kids will respond with the statement: "But Dad, all the guys at school can say it." Which may in fact be true. But, if the term is not OK in your home, it's important to stick to your guns. "I understand you hear this word a lot. Many people choose to say it. However, we do not use it in this house. I don't want it said here again." You may even have to go so far as to explain: "Yes, Uncle Rob does say it. You still are not allowed to."

If your children are saying bad words in anger, let them know those phrases are unacceptable ways to express their feelings. Discuss more appropriate ways, such as taking a walk to get away from the situation, whalloping a punching bag, or using less aggressive words. If anger management is still a problem, seek the advice of a school counselor or other expert in child psychology.

If you notice a trend of poor language creeping into their vocabularies, don't be afraid to use more serious methods. The technique that works best for me is charging for bad words. I explain the process ahead of time, discuss the words that will be charged for and the amount of the fine. I levy the fine as soon as the word has been heard. But I don't allow tattling by siblings. Fees can range from 10 cents for younger children to

$1.00 for older kids. I also encourage the kids to listen to our words and fine us when we slip up!

One common practice I don't condone is washing a child's mouth out with soap. I believe the goal is to teach better verbal choices. Humiliating and physically violating a youngster only fosters aggression, and encourages the exact behavior parents are trying to be rid of.

Parental Self-Talk
Making Your Positive Inner Dialogue Work For You

Parental self-talk is the internal dialogue mothers and fathers conduct within themselves about their children and their parenting experiences. Self-talk can be either positive or negative. And it has a profound effect on how parents relate to their youngsters.

Positive self-talk may sound like this: "I don't like her tantrums, but I know they are only a phase;" "Other mothers I talk with say they sometimes feel overwhelmed, too;" and "It's hard to keep things tidy with young children in the house, but this clutter won't last forever."

Negative self-talk may sound like this: "It's been three months since my baby was born. My figure should be back to normal;" "These kids are driving me crazy. They never sit still for a minute!" or "I can't get any work done because my children can't do anything for themselves!"

Parental self-talk plays an enormous role in the feelings and behaviors parents exhibit with their youngsters. In fact, what parents *tell* themselves about what's happening with their children is more important than the actual events themselves. Positive self-talk helps them handle situations logically, calmly and patiently, and to experience greater satisfaction in their roles as moms and dads. Negative self-talk makes them feel angry, frustrated, inadequate and over burdened, and minimizes their enjoyment of their kids.

Let's say seventeen month-old Josh is dropping food onto the floor from his high chair. If you use negative self-talk and tell yourself, "That little brat. He always makes such a mess," you're apt to be impatient and short-tempered with him. You may feel compelled to scold him--or even spank him--for his behavior.

If, on the other hand, you use positive self-talk and say to yourself, "This little fellow looks as if he's done eating," you're more likely to calmly clear his plate and good-naturedly lift him out of his chair.

Most self-talk is learned. We hear our parents and other family members talk about their children, and we repeat that language to ourselves about our own families.

Self-talk is also habitual. Similar situations trigger the same internal messages. For example, whenever Judy's four year-old daughter, Caitlin, can't find one of her toys, Judy tells herself, "She's ungrateful and careless. She needs to learn how to be more responsible." She then lectures her daughter about taking better care of her possessions.

Fortunately, we can learn how to use positive self-talk to our advantage to improve our relationships with our children. Start by listening to the messages you tell yourself about your youngsters. Note if your thoughts are mostly positive or mostly negative.

Next, notice how you react to your self-talk. For instance, if you tell yourself, "I hate having to help my kids with their homework," you may find that you project a negative attitude toward school and your children's assignments.

Ask yourself how you would *like* to behave with your youngsters. If you want to demonstrate a value for education and learning, you'll want to teach your kids good study habits, and give nightly school work top priority.

Decide what statements you can say to yourself that increase the likelihood of your desired behavior. Perhaps you can tell yourself, "School wasn't emphasized in my household when I was growing up, but I want to do things differently. I know it will take determination. And I know I'll make some mistakes. But if I stick with my goals, I can give these kids opportunities that weren't available to me."

Use your new, positive self-talk often. In fact, the more frequently you repeat the messages, the sooner you'll elicit the desired behaviors and emotions.

You may find that you occasionally slip back into old, negative self-talk. Don't worry. It's been with you a long time and may feel as familiar as a worn pair of shoes. Simply remind yourself that change takes time and patience. Any progress you make will be beneficial to you and to your children.

Talking With Your Youngsters
A Mentally Stimulating Activity

Do today's parents talk enough to their children? Many of them don't. Between the demands of families, careers, fast-lane lifestyles and TV and video viewing, parents find increasingly less time to converse with their kids.

Talking to children serves a variety of important roles in their lives. First of all, talking teaches language. Children need to hear constant examples of spoken words for them to learn to speak.

Talking to children stimulates the development of their brains. Research shows that frequent mother-child verbal interaction is the primary factor for boosting children's mental abilities. Dr. Jane Healy, in her eye-opening book, *Endangered Minds*, describes how new experiences literally alter the structure of developing brains. By a process Dr. Healy terms "scaffolding," the brain is gradually enhanced as a result of on-going, age-appropriate stimulation.

Talking to children provides them with knowledge. They acquire facts about the world and how it functions. When Marcie talks with her two year-old daughter, Leesa, about the aquarium they see in the pet store, she can teach her about fish, bubbles, snails and water--all in a few minutes' time.

Talking to children enriches their vocabulary. And, since words are the backbone of thoughts, youngsters with wide varieties of words at their disposal are better equipped to express their thoughts and feelings.

Talking to children helps them solve problems. For instance, when Paul forgot his homework, he and his dad decided Paul should call a classmate and get the assignment. Paul not only completed the work, but also learned how to tackle new dilemmas.

Many parents erroneously believe television eliminates much of the need for moms and dads to talk with their children. They rationalize that educational shows, such as Sesame Street, can adequately prepare pre-schoolers for school by teaching them the alphabet or familiarizing them with their numbers.

Unfortunately, nothing could be further from the truth. According to Dr. Healy, most children's programming is presented in a disorganized manner, with sounds, shapes, colors and stories appearing haphazardly on the screen. The material can't be geared to each viewer's intellectual functioning, so youngsters are regularly bombarded with information they're not yet ready to absorb. And, since hyperstimulation is the norm for children's media, kids become better lookers than listeners, and may have difficulty paying attention in school.

What can you do to successfully talk with your child? Start as early as you can. Regularly "converse" with your infant. Discuss what you're doing with your toddler. He won't be able to answer yet, but you'll be stimulating him to talk.

Use your words to say what your youngster can't. If 18 month-old Allison is tired and fussy, gently inform her, "You are ready for your nap. We've had a busy morning playing in the snow."

Answer your child's questions. Sure, they can sometimes be tedious. But take the time to explain what your toddler is pointing to, or share in his wonder at his world.

If your child is in daycare, try to find English-speaking providers. Children who spend large amounts of time with non-English speaking adults have a more difficult time mastering the language. Look for daycare facilities where adults will be available to talk with your tot.

Finally, avoid correcting your young child's grammar. You want to stimulate conversation, not stifle it by making him feel self-conscious.

Instead, model appropriate speaking. Here's what I mean: Let's say six year-old Jesse bursts into the room, announcing, "Chris and I goed to the store!" Rather than correcting him--"No, Jesse. Don't say, 'Goed to the store,'"--say, "Hey! You and Chris went to the store, did you? Sounds like you're excited about that!" You'll be helping shape his language, while still encouraging him to talk.

Chapter 5

Stress And Anxiety

"Don't hurry and worry. You're only here for a short visit. So be sure to stop and smell the flowers."

Walter C. Hagen
1892-1969

Stress
Steps for Keeping It Under Control

Parents' lives are packed with change. Changing family structures, changing economic demands, changing developmental stages of our children...We are constantly forced to adapt.

Each of these adaptations is stressful. For example, we must rearrange our lifestyles to accommodate a teen-ager's growing need for independence. Or we must be ever vigilant to keep a newly walking toddler safe.

Even positive events induce stress. The discovery of a long-desired pregnancy moves a couple from the stresses of the fertility clinic into the changes associated with pregnancy, possible career adjustments and nursery decorations.

Certainly some events are more stressful than others. Caring for a seriously ill child, for instance, or handling a teen's drug problem are far more stressful than helping a child on a history project.

But, because stressful events are cumulative, even seemingly minor events can be too much. Changing hours at work, one child at home with the flu, a car in the repair shop and an argument with your spouse can shoot your stress levels through the roof. Suddenly, one innocent request--to bake cookies for the school picnic --seems overwhelming, and you fall apart at the seams.

But all stressful events, if left unchecked, can take their toll on our bodies and our lives. Stress has been found to be related to a myriad of physical ailments, from headaches to peptic ulcers and arthritis.

Overly stressed parents usually report feeling irritable and tired. They do and say things to their loved ones that they wouldn't do or say under calmer conditions. They don't enjoy their children or spouses. In short, they find little enjoyment in their lives.

High stress levels make us feel out of control. We're no longer in the driver's seat of our life, but rather chasing along behind the car.

You can help diminish stress by examining which areas you can regain control of. For example, let's say you have a new baby. You feel stressed and out of control because you can't get anything done during the day. You can't change your stage of life. But you may decide to do household chores during the baby's first nap, and put your feet up and read a magazine during the afternoon nap. You'll be taking care of both your family and yourself.

Set limits on your time. You can't do everything for every person in your life, including your kids. Limit your children to workable after school activities. Say "No" to other commitments you just can't take on.

Find solutions to stressful situations. One wise mom I know drastically cut the stress around her home in the evening by hiring a tutor to help her daughter with her homework. Mom didn't have to lock horns with Sis over her Geometry, and was freed up to help her other youngsters.

Keep realistic expectations about what you and your family should be doing. For instance, don't expect your five year-old to keep his room immaculate, or your toddler to sit quietly through dinner. Work with them as best you can, but don't develop an ulcer over their behavior.

Allow yourself plenty of time to relax and recharge. You can't do anything if your internal battery is drained. While high stress situations are the *least* conducive times for relaxation, they are the *most* important times to do so. Whether you take a walk, catch a movie, read a book or ride your bike, you'll be taking a positive step toward minimizing your stress.

Fast-Lane Families
Regaining Control of Your Schedule

Two friends, both mothers with several children, meet in the mall.

"How are you?" asks the first.

"Busy as ever," responds the second. "The kids are doing 4-H, soccer, dance, football, flute, karate and Youth Group. And you?"

"Life is crazy, crazy, crazy. I'm exhausted all the time. Got to go. Nice talking with you."

Today's "fast-lane families" are doing more and going faster than ever before. Unfortunately, they may be headed for some head-on collisions.

Our culture values "busy-ness." In fact, we equate being busy with being important. The more we get done, the more valuable we believe we are.

As a result, we cram more and more into our lives. Outcome doesn't matter. Activity does.

Fast-lane parents inflict this philosophy onto their children by signing them up for excessive numbers of lessons and activities. Monday is Spanish, Tuesday is scouts, Wednesday is tutoring and Thursday is tennis. The parents feel like maniacs, and the kids don't have a moment to breathe.

I certainly don't advocate sloth. But frenetic, fast paced lifestyles can create serious problems for family members.

Children growing up in fast-lane families never learn how to manage their time. They aren't encouraged to make choices between two equally enticing after-school activities. Instead, they're all crammed into the schedule.

Communication suffers when families do too much. Let's face it, talking takes time. It's impossible to carry on a conversation with someone when you're always dashing out the door.

When communication falters, family bonds weaken. It's hard to be close with people you don't know well. And busy, fast-lane families have less time to share themselves with each other.

Problems often aren't resolved adequately in fast-lane families. Those long, quiet parent-child talks, so necessary when kids are growing up, are less likely to happen within tight schedules. Issues get swept under the rug in hopes they'll go away.

Exhaustion and irritability are more prevalent when family members try to do too much. It's hard to be loving and reasonable when you're always pooped.

How can you tell if your family's in the fast-lane? Listen to yourself talk. Do you regularly complain to your friends that you are too busy? Do you often put off your children with the excuse, "I'm too busy right now"?

Notice how you feel. Do you wish you could cancel everything and hibernate for a week?

Finally, watch your kids. Do they have lots of time to play by themselves or with friends? Or are they on perpetual treadmills so that they make it to all of their activities?

If you find you're a fast-lane family, let go of unnecessary demands. I know they all feel important, and you don't want to shirk on your commitments. But it's more important to get your lives under control than to live up to every one else's expectations.

Make a conscious effort to operate at a slower pace. It will feel odd at first, but it really is OK to leave some hours unscheduled.

Set aside large chunks of unstructured time to be together as a family. You might head for the park or simply sit around the fire. Whatever you choose, don't be afraid to be together without a commitment. After all, the most important activity you can do is to spend time with the people you love.

Beating The "Way-Too-Much-To-Do Blues"

Let's see...the kids have basketball, dance, cheerleading and drums. The baby is recovering from the chicken pox. My husband's parents are coming this weekend. And my boss needs me to work overtime. Help! I've got the "Way-too-much-to-do Blues!"

The "Way-too-much-to-do Blues" strikes conscientious parents of all ages who want to be successful in every endeavor. Whether they're in the office, classroom or home, such mothers and fathers strive to do their best professionally and personally, giving unselfishly of their time and resources. They help Junior finish his fourth grade California mission project, oversee Sister's ballet recital and volunteer for every committee at their temple. Unfortunately, they often feel over burdened, unappreciated, irritable and exhausted.

Most "WTMTD Blues" sufferers rationalize that if they had more time during the day, their lives wouldn't be so chaotic. "If I only didn't have to sleep," one Blues patient told me. "Then I could get everything done."

What these over-doers fail to recognize is this disease is a long-time habit, an addiction if you will. People who over load their lives don't stop when they've done enough. They just add more to do. Give them a few more hours, and they jam in more activities.

How can you tell if you're afflicted? Ask yourself the following questions:

* Do you wake up in the morning feeling behind schedule?

* Do you say, "Hurry up," to your kids more than five times a day?

* Does every conversation with your friends revolve around how busy you are?

* Are you crabby from morning until night?

* Does your spouse only half-jokingly call you Attila?

If you answered "yes," to most of these questions, then you've got the "WTMTD Blues"--bad!

But don't despair. There is hope. First, recognize this pattern at work in your life. Notice your tendency to pack more into your day than you can possibly do. Allow yourself to feel how uncomfortable you make your life, and the lives of those around you.

Evaluate your choices of activities and see which can be eliminated. Some parts of your day, such as taking care of young children or going to work, are automatic. You can't do much to change them. But others, such as how much time you donate to an organization, are more flexible, and may even need to be put on hold until you're in a different time in your life.

Don't let your kids' schedules drive you crazy. There are a zillion activities your children can be involved in. And each is sure to be fun and beneficial in some way. But children are much better off with calm parents than they are doing five or six things after school every week. Perhaps you decide to limit each child to one activity. Or you select activities that meet only on the weekends. Whatever you do, find a solution that will keep you sane.

Schedule relaxation time for yourself as conscientiously as you schedule the rest of your day. Many busy parents feel guilty if they play tennis once a week instead of doing chores, or if they spend an evening with their buddies instead of working late. The truth is that you need "down time" as much as you need sleep and food. Resting is not a sign of weakness. It's a sign of someone who is able to maintain a balanced lifestyle. Remember, even God rested on the seventh day.

There's no denying that life with children is busy. But if you can pick and choose where you use your time, you may find yourself whistling a happier tune instead of singing the blues.

Kicking The Rush-Rush Routine

"I'm always late!" moaned Ellen, a busy mother of three children under seven years of age. "I constantly feel anxious. My kids will even point out to me, 'Mom, you're driving like a maniac.'"

Lateness is an ongoing issue for parents. Kids are demanding, unpredictable and always changing. One tot's nap you could normally set your watch by, runs 45 minutes longer on the day you've scheduled your tax appointment. The ten-minute drive to your son's tutor was stretched to thirty when you had to drive back to school to retrieve his forgotten homework.

Of course, some lateness is inevitable. When your baby spits up breakfast on the way to church, you must go back home and change her. And when your kindergartener declares, "I have to go to the bathroom," as you're loading the family in the car, you have no choice but to wait.

But some parents make tardiness a pattern. Although they usually complain about their perpetual lack of punctuality, they actually feel comfortable with their constant states of anxiety and guilt.

For example, Beth always arrived twenty minutes late. She was regularly dressed and ready to leave on time. But when she noticed she was still so early, she would start another project. By the time the new activity was completed, she was behind schedule, and ready to leave.

Arriving early felt strange to Beth. Hurrying felt much better.

Want to break out of the rush-rush routine? Start by consciously making promptness a priority. Decide you no longer want to have a hurried and anxious lifestyle, and that you're willing to take the steps to make it possible.

Look at your schedule. Are you trying to accomplish too much? If so, give yourself permission to let go of "overdo-itis." Contrary to your expectations, you're not super human. You have limits to your stamina, time and patience.

Dick suffered from this problem. His two daughters lived with him from Thursday until Sunday every week. He was determined to help them with their school work, personally drive them to their activities and take them to their doctors' appointments. But he also wanted to get in as much time as possible at work.

As a result of trying to do so much, Dick often arrived too late to take the girls where they needed to go, and was too rushed to enjoy them when they were with him. It wasn't until he set limits, both at work and with his daughters, that he finally gained control of his life.

When you have an appointment, make a schedule for yourself. Let's say 18 month-old Porter has to go to the doctor at eleven this morning. The office is ten minutes away, so you count back ten minutes for the time you'll have to leave.

Porter takes thirty minutes to dress and get in his car seat, so you count back another half an hour to find the time you'll have to start getting him ready. Add time to feed him breakfast and get yourself showered. Then, put an additional fifteen minutes into the schedule to allow for any last minute phone calls or mishaps.

I can already hear you complaining: "If I have to schedule myself so far back each day, I'll only get one thing done!" And sometimes that's the case! Especially when you're dealing with very young children, some days go by when very little is accomplished other than caring for that child or going to the store.

What gets most parents into trouble is expecting they'll be able to do much more.

Give older children specific instructions about when you want them to be ready and what you want them to do. Then give them a ten minute warning before you're walking out the door. Check on them five minutes before departure to move along any stragglers.

Your kids won't necessarily support your new-found promptness. But by making punctuality a priority, you'll not only be providing them with a good role model, you'll be teaching them skills that will serve them the rest of their lives.

Morning Mayhem
Making Mornings More Serene

Morning mayhem. We all know the scene. Nurse and change the baby. Fix oatmeal for little Jake. Help Elisa track down her bike helmet. And get Paul off to work. Meanwhile, prepping yourself to face whatever professional and personal tasks you tackle during your day.

But conquering morning mayhem means more than winning a daily round of "Beat the Clock." It also involves creating a nurturing atmosphere that equips family members to meet their days. Let's face it, none of us are much good if we're met with yelling and excessive tension before we even leave home.

To minimize morning mayhem, start by establishing a routine. The more you and your brood do out of habit, the less you'll have to think about in the morning. For example, have kids put their lunches in the same place every day after school. Install pegs for hanging bike helmets, jackets and backpacks. Clear the top drawer for the bus pass. Do everything you can to minimize frantic, last minute searches for those must-have-before-leaving items.

Set a time schedule and stick to it. Decide when the kids need to be up, how long they have to eat their breakfasts, when they brush their teeth and when they're out the door. Allow enough time for everyone to stay calm, but don't cave in to their pleadings. (I know my own kids would eat breakfast until noon if I let them.)

You may warrant the nickname Atilla, but it's kinder than going ballistic because they've missed the bus.

In our family, the children are up by 7:30, dressed and eating breakfast by 7:45, brushing their teeth and combing their hair by 8:00, and out the door by 8:15. This schedule includes a small amount of dawdle, wrestle-with-your-brother leeway. But if I let them get too side-tracked, chaos soon ensues.

If you have a child with a special morning need, allow extra time in your routine. When my older son started first grade, he missed having time to play quietly in the morning. We worked out a schedule that gave him twenty extra minutes to build with his Leggos before catching the bus.

Do as much as possible the night before. Lay out young children's clothes, shoes and hair ribbons. Have older children pack homework and projects in their backpacks. Prepare bottles for the baby for daycare. Even pre-pack lunch pails with carrot sticks, cartons of fruit juice, granola bars and cheese--all do-ahead types of foods.

Elicit older kids' help to minimize morning hassles. Hold a family meeting and ask, "It's important that I get to work on time. And I know no one likes it when I blow my stack. What can I count on you girls doing to make things go smoothly?" Then, lay out a plan together for everyone to follow.

Don't expect your younger children to be able to follow through without getting side-tracked. Stop at regular intervals to make sure they're getting dressed and making their beds. Yelling at them only adds stress, and often makes them go even slower. Gentle supervision of bed making and teeth brushing is more effective.

Don't expect very young children to help you meet your obligations. I remember one mother bemoaning the fact her three year-old kept making her late: "No matter how much I explain to Todd that I have an important meeting, he doesn't seem to listen." This mom needed to realize that getting Todd out of the house was her responsibility, not the other way around.

Finally, try to send family members out the door with a kind word. A heartfelt, "I love you," or "Have a great day," gives them one last shot of encouragement to help them face their obligations.

Taking Five
A Valuable Technique When You Lose Your Cool

Losing your patience with your children? Feeling like you want to throttle your pre-schooler, go ballistic with your grade-schooler or put your teen on the next bus out of town? Then take five, back off from the situation and go away until you've cooled off.

Any place will work. You can retreat to your bedroom, take a walk, hit a punching bag, jog on the beach or pull weeds. I've even known parents who locked themselves in their bathrooms when they started to lose their cool. Wherever you go, make it clear to your son or daughter, "I'm too angry to talk about this now. We'll discuss it when I'm calmer."

Taking five lets you regain control of both yourself and the situation. It demonstrates to your child you're still in authority, and you're exercising that authority by temporarily backing away.

Taking five lets you analyze what's going on. Why are you so upset? What can you do about it? You can't think rationally in the midst of an emotional tempest. Taking five and regaining your composure is the only way.

Tish often felt her blood boil while she was trying to toilet train two year-old Jerome. He refused to sit on the new potty chair she had purchased. And he consistently kicked at her and cried when she attempted to lift him onto it. She was so frustrated she wanted to spank him. Instead, she decided to take five and think about her dilemma. When she did, she realized Jerome wasn't ready to learn to use the toilet. She wisely opted to forego any further training for at least six months.

Taking five prevents you from doing or saying something physically or emotionally hurtful to your child. You disengage from the conflict rather than make it worse.

Let's say your ten month-old baby is teething, and her constant crying is driving you nuts. Instead of yelling at her, or shaking her in frustration--and possibly doing serious damage--you make sure she is safely in her crib, then you close the door to her room and walk outside for five minutes. When you have calmed down, you return to her room, take a deep, soothing breath, and gently carry her to the rocker to sing her a song.

Taking five lets you regroup and develop a strategy for handling the problem. Do you need a break from your twin toddlers? Do you need to problem-solve with your high schooler? Taking five is the time to lay out that next step.

Finally, taking five models great problem-solving skills for your children. Seeing mom and dad backing off when they're upset teaches kids the same coping tactic. They'll be less likely to get into squabbles at school or lose their tempers when they get hot under the collar.

How can you tell if you need to take five? Pay attention to your body. If you feel relaxed and free from excess muscle tension in your face, stomach or hands, you're probably OK. If, on the other hand, your muscles are tense, your hands are clenched or your jaw is tightly clamped, you're probably ready to explode. That's the time to retreat from the scene until you're less upset.

Ted had difficulty controlling his temper with his teen-age daughter, Becca. Whenever she was demanding or rude, his stomach tied up in knots and his hands clenched into fists. He felt the urge to yell, "Grow up! You're not the only one in this house!" But when he did lose control, she swore at him, then ran away in tears. He knew he wasn't handling her well, but his anger got in the way.

Then, Ted tried a new strategy. When Becca said something inflammatory, and he wanted to scream in her face, he took a deep breath and said, "Becca, I'm not going to listen to those words. If you want to talk to me politely, I'll consider what you're saying." If his daughter continued to harangue him, he simply left the room. This didn't eliminate all of his daughter's unpleasant behavior, of course. But it did put Ted back in control of himself and the situation.

Guilt
Don't Let It Run Your Life

Guilt is every parent's enemy. It makes them feel bad about themselves, incompetent in dealing with their children and miserable in their roles as parents.

Guilt can be brought on by mistakes a parent made in the past. For instance, Madeline felt guilty because she didn't make her son, Casey, wear a bike helmet the day he was involved in a serious accident.

Parents can feel guilty about decisions they make, and how those decisions affect their children. Laura felt guilty about leaving her eight week-old infant with a sitter while she went back to her job.

External pressures cause other parents to feel guilty. Dave felt guilty because he wasn't able to earn enough money at his job to buy the home he felt his in-laws expected him to provide for their daughter.

Other parents experience guilt as a normal state, even when they have nothing in particular to feel guilty about. Marcy felt particularly anxious when Jason was born. She constantly worried that she wouldn't be a competent mother, even though her pediatrician regularly assured her that she was doing fine.

Parents are acutely susceptible to guilt. They must make countless decisions about their families' well-being. They inherently make mistakes as they learn about their developing children, and as their families change and grow. They feel overly responsible for their youngsters' success in life. And, finally, they must handle our culture's penchant for blaming parents when problems arise.

Guilt manifests itself in a wide variety of ways. Some people experience anxiety, restlessness, muscle tension and insomnia. Others report overwhelming feelings of inadequacy or failure.

However it is felt, the results are the same. Continuous guilt saps parents' precious mental and physical resources. They have less energy to handle their regular stresses. They wind up exhausted, emotionally burned out and feeling more guilty than ever about not being able to keep up with their daily chores.

What many parents fail to realize is that their guilt serves no constructive purpose. Rather than harnessing the energy generated by their guilt to make some positive changes in their lives, most parents simply use it to make themselves feel rotten.

Fortunately, you don't have to be a guilt-plagued parent. You can recognize guilt as a destructive force in your life, and take concrete steps to get rid of it.

Allow yourself to be human. Parenting is not a perfect process. We all make mistakes--many of them. Use your goofs as lessons about how to handle something next time. And know that you are teaching your own kids how to recover from their slips.

No decisions--especially those involving families--are 100 per cent. All that you can do is make the best choice you can, based on the knowledge available to you at the moment.

No matter how you decide on an issue, part of you will be pleased, and part of you will be disappointed.

You can still have internal conflict without feeling guilty about doing the wrong thing.

Rick and Patty were trying to decide if they should hold their daughter back for another year in kindergarten. They weighed all the data, discussed the matter with the appropriate school personnel, then opted to move her into first grade. They realized their decision was not perfect, but they knew it was the best they could make.

Helping Children Manage Their Anger

All children get angry. Physical limitations, siblings, school, friends and parents are common sources of childhood anger. But while anger may be a normal reaction, kids need to be taught safe and appropriate ways of expressing it.

Anger must never be manifested in a violent or physically abusive manner. Kids should never be allowed to hit, scratch or in any way harm another person's body or property.

The same holds true for verbal abuse. Contrary to popular psychological writing of the '70's and '80's, that encouraged people to engage in no-holds-barred vocal fisticuffs when angry, emotional lashings do more harm than good. Kids need to know that yelling at or verbally demeaning someone is not an acceptable outlet for their anger.

When children feel angry enough to verbally or physically lash out at someone, they should be encouraged to take five and back away from the situation until they have cooled down. Having youngsters go to their bedrooms, or similar quiet environments, helps them regain control of themselves, avoid doing something harmful and collect their thoughts about what happened.

Guide kids into safe expressions of their anger. Very young children can hit stuffed animals or pillows. They can re-enact the upsetting event with dolls or toys, giving voices to the characters, and taking actions they couldn't do in real life. Older children can hit punching bags, write stories about their feelings or take long walks.

One creative children's book, *Mean Soup,* by Betsy Everitt, tells how a mother and son yell into the steam of a boiling pot of broth as they add the soup's ingredients.

Young children often have difficulty identifying their anger, so you can help them describe their feelings and reach a solution. For instance, you may help a preschooler verbalize the following thoughts: "You are angry, Jesse, because Tommy took that toy. Can you use your words to tell Tommy how you feel and how you'd please like your toy back?"

Model appropriate responses to anger. For example, you can replace spanking or yelling with such statements as, "I'm too angry to talk with you right now. I'll get back to you when I've calmed down."

Of course, none of us are saints. We all slip up and do and say things we regret later. By honestly admitting you've made a mistake while angry, you'll be sharing your humanness with your youngsters, and demonstrating a wonderful way of handling problems.

While anger is a normal reaction to a situation, uncontrollable outbursts are not. If you, or other family members, are troubled by ongoing anger, family counseling may be able to help.

Finally, avoid becoming embroiled in your kids' emotional outbursts. Shouting matches seldom accomplish anything except hoarse voices and hurt feelings. Instead, let them know you hear they are very angry, and that you'll respond when they're under control. When young children are upset, talk to them very softly so they must quiet themselves to hear your voice.

Hovering
Letting Go of Excessive Parental Concern

Hovering is the excessive concern many parents have over their children's well-being. It's a parenting style of the '90's. And it's not doing our kids any good.

Hovering is characterized by an obsessive need to provide children with a wrinkle-free existence. It assumes kids shouldn't have to adapt to their surroundings, that life instead should be absent of almost all responsibility and concern.

Parents who hover also tend to feel a lot of guilt about how they're raising their children. They worry about the amount of time they spend with them, how they're doing in school, about the activities their youngsters are involved in, and whether their kids have high enough self-esteem.

A subtle competition even arises among such parents to see who can care the very most about their offspring. Moms and dads doing less than the established norm are quietly labeled inadequate, while those hovering the most are admired for their concern.

Of course, we all want to do what's best for our sons and daughters. No one would advocate neglecting them. But hovering is unique to our generation, and it's carrying parental concern to the extreme.

As one would expect, this parenting style is most common in families with only one or two children, who live in relatively affluent areas. Let's face it, families with lots of mouths to feed, or who are scraping to make ends meet, just can't afford the luxury of hovering over their youngsters.

But today's pampered progeny may actually be at a disadvantage. More material goods are being heaped upon them, while less is being expected of them in terms of chores and general responsibilities. Because hovering protects them from having to get along in a variety of adverse situations, these boys and girls are less prepared to solve problems and get along with others as they grow up.

Children who are hovered over also assume that the rest of the world will coddle and care for them in the same precious manner they are being raised. Anyone living and working on his own soon realizes this isn't the case.

How can you tell if you are the hovering type? Ask yourself the following questions:

1) Do you ask to interview teachers at your child's school to make sure they're a good fit with your son or daughter?

2) Do you often feel your child is being treated unfairly by her teachers, coaches, den leaders or other youth leaders?

3) Do you feel the need to help your child solve problems with friends?

4) Do you rush back to school when your child forgets work, rather than let him face the consequences in the morning?

5) Do you feel you're not raising your child right?

If you answered, "yes," to most of these questions, then you're probably a hovering parent. But don't despair. It's never too late to back off.

Realize it's OK for your children to have some problems. That's how kids learn to solve them. Providing a loving back-up system allows them to experiment with what works and what doesn't.

Talk about strategies for dealing with difficult people and situations. For example, you might role-play how to handle the playground bully.

Use the following phrase often: "That's your problem. You'll need to take care of it." You'll be empowering your kids to control their own lives, while helping them develop the skills to do it.

Don't Overdo For Your Kids
Their Lives Needn't Be Three-Ring Circuses

Attention other parents: I no longer care if my kids are having fun. I hereby rid myself of the need to have eternally happy children.

This decision has been in the making for a while. I realized that what made my two sons happy one day was not necessarily what made them happy the next. Yesterday they wanted Leggos, today it's a brand new bike.

Even if something did capture their attentions for more than a weekend, it was soon to be new and improved. Computer games and technical wizardry change faster than the pages in my date book, with each generation of gizmodoodles claiming thrills and entertainment unheard of one month before.

The old stuff was--Heaven forbid!--boring. They wanted the newest and the best.

I ended up feeling resentful. Not only was I running my tail off trying to please them, but nothing I did seemed to work. I felt used and unappreciated. And I behaved like the Wicked Witch of the West.

Then one day I asked them, "So guys, what really makes you happy?" Their responses opened my eyes. "Pizza each evening for dinner. No homework, no school and no chores."

I knew right then I'd been going at it all wrong. Inherent in their desire to be happy was an absence of anything that would help them develop character.

Happiness also meant no responsibilities, either to themselves or anyone else. I would actually be doing my children a disservice if I allowed them to follow their urges to have perpetual fun.

Let's say I denied my boys the chance to do household chores. They'd miss out on the feelings of being valuable and necessary members of our family. They wouldn't experience the satisfaction that comes with seeing a difficult task through to completion. They'd lose out on the development of family cohesion.

Or maybe they wouldn't have to keep their rooms clean or mop up after themselves in the kitchen. They'd say that would make them happy. But in just a few years they'll be forced to take care of themselves. What a tragedy if they *still* expect others to care for them, rather than being able to fend for themselves.

So I've established new goals for my youngsters. I now value their feelings of competence over their immediate feelings of happiness. I want them to develop confidence about who they are and what they can do.

I want them to make good decisions, and feel secure about their choices. I'm concerned more about their long-range maturity than about their short-term enjoyment.

This is certainly not to say I want my kids to be miserable. Believe me, I *love* watching them have fun. Nothing gives me greater pleasure than seeing my boys and a battalion of companions chasing up and down the hills near our home.

Fun is an integral part of our family life, too. We all have a great time together backpacking, skiing, reading stories and playing games.

The difference is I'm no longer a slave to their every entertainment whim. Just as I denied them candy when they were babies because I knew it wasn't good for them, I now set limits on their possessions and behaviors for exactly those same reasons.

We parents are older and wiser than our children so we can guide them with knowledge and insight they haven't yet acquired. By helping kids get a grip on their impulses, and letting them discover the rewards inherent in their success, we'll turn lives filled with non-stop "grabbing gimmes" into lives full of satisfaction and joy.

Helping Your Children Manage Frustration

Craig is frustrated--again. Although bright and capable, this eight year-old is reduced to tears and feelings of failure whenever he falls short of his own high expectations. His parents are equally concerned about what they can do to help their only child with this problem.

While all children become frustrated with themselves at times, some can be emotionally paralyzed by their inabilities to handle relatively insignificant problems in their lives. Such children may be perfectionists, and are often first-born or only children.

The solution to helping kids handle their frustrations involves a two-pronged approach. First, control their environments as much as possible to minimize frustrating situations. Make sure toys are age-appropriate for younger tots, and remove those that regularly cause distress.

Encourage your child to select activities that are emotionally suitable to her learning style. For example, if your girl is a whiz on the baseball diamond, but frustrated to tears at the piano, let her spend more time on the mound, and less time at the ivories.

Set realistic standards for your child. If you're hypercritical of your youngster, he's more likely to be critical of himself. Support his efforts over his results; the goal is to study hard for the spelling test, not necessarily get 100%.

Second, teach your child how to better handle his frustration. One technique, taking five, involves setting the difficult task aside for a few minutes until he's calmer. Let him know that he won't solve anything if his stomach is tied in knots, and he's ready to rip up his homework. Having a snack, reading a book, doing another assignment or taking a walk are all good ways to let go of the frustration, and approach it later with a clearer head.

Deep breathing is another good skill. When tensions mount, simply relax your shoulders, close your eyes and tune in to your breathing. You may even count your slow breaths, feeling yourself relax with each one.

Both of these exercises can be done at home or in the classroom, and can be easily taught to kids.

When dealing with children who have lost their cool, it's important for parents to stay calm, and not become angry themselves. The child is already out of control; the last thing she needs is a parent in the same state.

Talk softly. Your quiet voice will not only help soothe the child, but she'll have to stop crying to listen to what you're saying. Encourage the child to gain control of herself: "Jessica, I know you're angry, but you need to calm down." If you're dealing with a young child, you may try to distract her, and involve her in another activity: "Here, let's put this puzzle away for now. How about looking at this book?" Quietly reading a story (even whispering it) works wonders in regaining calm.

Encourage an older child to analyze the problem. If he can't tell you what's wrong, ask gentle, probing questions: "James, can you tell me what's going on? Is it a problem understanding your homework?" Explore solutions: "Do you not understand this assignment? Shall we look in your book?" Encourage him to stay in control; let him know that you'll help him, but he must stop crying. Share the above calming techniques. When he does finally regain control, acknowledge his ability to do so.

Parents can do their best to help youngsters cope with frustrations. But they need to recognize that the problem ultimately belongs to the children. While moms and dads may try to minimize stresses and teach coping skills, the kids are the ones who must face their personal styles of relating to their worlds, and devise their own solutions.

Teaching Kids About Safety
Power is Better Than Paranoia

Many parents are increasingly paranoid about their children's safety. Some refuse to let their children walk home from school for fear they'll be abducted. Others severely curtail their youngsters' normal neighborhood explorations, dreading the presence of a lurking maniac.

This is not to say that some real dangers don't exist, or that we don't have to teach our children basic principles of safety. Nothing could be further from the truth.

But paranoid parenting doesn't make for safer children. In fact, causing kids to feel frightened, insecure and vulnerable only increases the likelihood they will become victims. The actual odds of a child being abducted are miniscule; however, the chances that same child will be paralyzed with fear by overly protective parents are great.

How can you avoid being a paranoid parent, and decrease the likelihood your son or daughter will be a victim?

Start by letting them know you feel confident in their abilities to care for themselves. As they grow, provide lots of chances for them to make important decisions for themselves, then reward them for their wise decisions. For example, you might tell your five year-old daughter that she chooses delightful friends to play with. Or you might acknowledge that your twelve year-old son has a big decision to make about whether or not to try out for the track team, then entrust him to make the right decision for himself. You'll be helping to instill a strong sense of self-confidence--the first line of defense.

Support your children's perceptions of other people. If one of your kids says that someone's parents were creepy, and he'd rather not spend the night, trust his judgment. Let him know he's making a smart decision in not staying some place he is uncomfortable.

Applaud your youngsters when they make a smart safety decision. For instance, you might praise your child when he acts wisely when he's lost: "Daniel, you did just the right thing when you got separated from me in the store. You stayed where you were and let me come back and find you. You really used your head." Had Daniel not acted so wisely--let's say he left the store in a panic looking for you--explain a safer alternative to him, then let him know he'll be able to handle himself better the next time something similar happens.

Discuss and practice safety and emergency procedures with your kids. Talk about what they should do if a stranger tries to give them candy, asks them to get into the car with him, or in any other way makes them feel unsafe. Decide who your children can call for help if they become frightened and you're not home. Discuss the options your youngsters have for finding safety in a neighborhood other than their own.

Lay out clear boundaries for where your kids can play, rules for letting you know where they are, and explicit times for them to be home.

Limit kids' exposure to violent television shows. Programs portraying childhood abductions, or other states of danger, only feed young viewers' insecurities.

Children need all the power they can get. We must, therefore, empower them with self-confidence, not imperil them with vulnerability. By turning paranoid youngsters into powerful ones, you'll be greatly boosting their chances for safety.

Managing Children's Varying Time Demands

"I'm frustrated," a mother recently told me. "I have to spend so much time with Darren, I feel I'm ignoring my other children."

It's not uncommon for one child to be more demanding of a family's time and resources than another. Perhaps a son has learning difficulties and requires extra help with his school work. A daughter might have a medical condition that necessitates many visits to the doctor.

You may even have a tot with a particularly demanding personality, who controls far more of his parents' time than his siblings.

Whatever the reason, the outcome is the same: one youngster needs more parental time than another, causing Mom and Dad to add guilt to the overload they're already carrying.

The problem, however, isn't with the situation. There's nothing inherently bad about a youngster with asthma, attention deficit or poor hearing. These conditions are simply given, just as is the child's gender, ethnicity and body type.

What *is* wrong is when the parents assume they should give the same amount of time to each of their children.

Contrary to the United States Constitution, all kids are not created equal. They demand from their environments at different rates. Just as it would be silly to assume a person 6'3" tall would require the same amount of food as someone 5'3" tall, it would be inane to think kids with differing physical or emotional issues would need the same amounts of their parents' time.

Now, I'm certainly not saying parents should ignore their other offspring in favor of the more demanding child. Rather, I'm encouraging them to carefully manage their daily 24 hours, and let go of the guilt that they're not super human. Recognize everyone in the family will adapt to the situation as best they can.

Let me give you an example. Let's say your toddler, Kate, has just been diagnosed with severe air-borne allergies, and you've been directed to eliminate as much mold and pollen from her room as possible.

You buy her new bedding, an air filter and an inhaler. And you spend hours reading about childhood allergies.

Her older brother, Michael, is free from any medical conditions, is doing well in school and is on his way to an apparently healthy, normal childhood.

But, rather than chastising yourself for spending more time on one child than another, you take a rational, self-supportive approach.

First, acknowledge your limits of solving your daughter's condition. Sure, you want to care for her as best you can. But excessive worry and over concern make little difference in how she feels, and drain you of all your resources.

Set aside regular time for your other child. You may choose to help out in his classroom one morning a week, or play ball with him on the weekends.

Take time for yourself. You're no good for anybody if you're constantly exhausted. Give yourself permission to relax, work-out, take a day off, read a book or visit friends.

Work with your spouse. Stressful children can easily take their toll on a relationship. Support each others' efforts to cope with the situation.

Turn your situation into a positive learning experience for your family. Should your other youngsters complain about all the fuss over a demanding sibling, respond calmly, "I know Kate requires lots of our time. But we take care of her because we love her, and that's what families do for each other."

You can even reassure him with the statement, "Michael, if you were the one needing special care, we would do just as much for you, too."

When You're A Less-Than-Perfect Parent

Sometimes I'm a perfect parent. I find just the right words to pacify battling siblings, or possess enough reassurance to calm a frightened nightmare victim back to sleep.

But sometimes I really blow it. I do and say things to my youngsters I regret for months to come. I switch from the persona of Mother Theresa to a character from a Stephen King horror novel.

The difference seldom lies with the children, but rather with what else is going on in my life. If I'm well rested, caught up on my chores and on time to my commitments, I can parent like a champ. But if my husband and I have quarreled, if the bank has lost a deposit slip or if I'm feeling over worked, I'm much more likely to snap.

Let me give you an example. I enjoy cooking my family's breakfast and helping them get to school and work on time. When my sons dawdle, I can usually move them along using humor and gentle nudging.

But one morning I had an important breakfast meeting, and I'd overslept. My family was still the same, but my perception wasn't as rosy. That morning I dashed crazily around the kitchen throwing breakfasts and lunches together, chastising them for being slobs and lecturing them on the need to take care of themselves. When the boys did their usual dawdling, I hit the roof, threatened to ground them for the month and practically threw them out the door.

Now, I'm certainly not condoning physically or psychologically hurting children. Nothing could be further from the truth. But let's face it. We parents make mistakes. Sometimes we goof big time.

The key is to learn how to minimize the chances of making those mistakes, and how to handle them more successfully after they've occurred.

Start by recognizing how your daily events effect the way you relate to your kids. Good days mean you've got more energy to deal with their issues. Bad days mean you have less in reserve to tackle their squabbles, spills at the table or lost homework assignments.

Count to ten before you handle your children or their problems. Don't respond too quickly. Give yourself a breather so you won't do or say something you regret.

Let's say your four year-old has spilled grape juice on the sofa, and you have company coming in an hour. Rather than yelling at him for being clumsy, you take a deep breath, count slowly to ten and say, "OK, Robert. Let's get this cleaned up."

Don't blame your kids for your short temper. They're not having the problem--you are. Avoid statements like, "You are driving me crazy today!" Instead, let them know you're having a tough day. Even a toddler can grasp the meaning in the words, "Mommy's really tired now. I can use lots of your help."

When you do lose your cool, apologize. Admit to them, "I blew it. I've been really frustrated today, but I know that's not your fault." You'll be re-establishing your parent-child communication, as well as providing a role model for them to follow when *they* make mistakes.

View your testiness as a warning signal. Perhaps you've taken on too many activities, or need more help with your chores. Maybe you have a time-management problem you've avoided solving. Whatever the solution, don't let this caution go unchecked.

Finally, if you're constantly feeling short-tempered with your children, or are afraid you are going to lose control of yourself and harm them, get help. Don't wait until it's too late. Parenting classes and trained counselors can improve your communication skills, teach new techniques for changing your kids' behavior, and provide you with much needed support.

Chapter 6

School Work And Education

"Education has for its object the formation of character."

Herbert Spencer
1820-1903

Raising Smart Children

Want to raise smart children? Start with these 10 steps:

<u>Be curious about life with your children</u>. Watch a spider build a web outside your toddler's window. Read a book about volcanoes to your kindergartner. Visit a dairy with your seven year-old. Or study roadbuilding equipment working along the interstate. You'll not only be broadening your youngster's base of knowledge, but you'll be nurturing an attitude of, "Life is interesting. I want to learn more about it."

<u>Take your children on family outings</u>. The museum, a children's concert, an art exhibit and a ghost town are only a few of the mentally stimulating activities you can use to enrich your youngsters' minds. Whether you travel across town or across the country, family outings have the added advantage of building your family's bonds as well as your kids' brains.

<u>Include your children in thought-provoking discussions</u>. Talk with your kids about current events, religion or school policies. It's a great way to learn their opinions, and a good method to develop their critical and analytical thinking. Avoid the temptation to prove your point or win every debate with your children. The goal is to help your kids formulate and express ideas, not necessarily change their views.

<u>Read to your children</u>. It's never too early to start reading to your tots. Even baby's enjoy listening to stories and looking at pictures. They'll learn to view

reading as a positive, relaxing activity. And they'll love the time you spend holding them in your arms.

Minimize their exposure to television and video games. There's a strong, negative correlation between children's success in school and the amount of TV they watch; a high score in one area almost always means a low score in the other. Encourage alternative, fun activities, such as playing games, riding bikes, working puzzles or reading books.

Help your children develop interesting hobbies. Raising tropical fish, building models, collecting stamps and playing the guitar are all examples of stimulating, mind-enhancing activities. Your youngsters will have fun as they're developing their powers of concentration, determination and patience.

Provide a structured environment for your children. Your home needn't run like a boot camp. But clear guidelines for behavior, regular meal times, on-going chore assignments and pre-determined study times and bedtimes teach kids how to manage their schedules, and gives them a sense of consistency in their lives.

Be active in your children's school work. Attend parent-teacher conferences. Support your school's P.T.A. Ask your kids what they're studying in Social Studies. Be available to help with homework. You'll be sending them a powerful message: "I care about your education."

Support your children's strengths. Let's face it. Not all of us are meant to be brain surgeons. And not all kids will be super students. Help your youngsters develop their natural talents and interests, and value their successes out of the classroom as well as in.

Muriel and Jack did this with their daughter, Kelly. Kelly had trouble in school, but had a wonderful gift for working with animals. Her parents encouraged her to participate in a local 4-H chapter, where she flourished with her dairy and poultry projects.

Kelly's 4-H successes eventually transferred to the classroom. She started to read more in order to learn about her heifer. And knowledge she gained while marketing her animals helped Kelly with her math.

<u>Value knowledge, education and success in your household</u>. Make learning and individual achievement top priorities in your home. Praise your kids for being diligent in their homework. Learn new vocabulary words together as a family. You'll be supporting their intellectual development, and setting them on the road to personal success.

Your Children's Education
10 Tips for Helping Them be Succesful

W ant to help your kids do their best in school this year? Start with these ten suggestions:

1) <u>Make school a top priority</u>. School is your youngsters' job. Let them know you think it's important. You can do it verbally by encouraging them to stay in school. Or you can give non-verbal messages by attending parent-teacher conferences and back-to-school nights.

2) <u>Set aside regular homework time</u>. It doesn't matter whether they study after school or after dinner. The key is that they develop a routine.

3) <u>Institute a quiet time in the evening</u>. Turn off the television, the video game and the stereo for a period of time each night. You'll be helping your children focus on their school work, and limiting potential diversions. This is especially important when only one person in the family is in school. Encouraging other family members to work or read silently not only supports the lone student, but gets younger brothers and sisters into the quiet study habit.

4) <u>Limit television and video game time</u>. It's no surprise that the best students watch the least TV. In fact, G.P.A.'s would sore if kids stayed away from the tube altogether from Monday through Friday. Your youngsters will be less distracted, and they'll be more likely to read books.

5) <u>Keep in contact with your children's teachers</u>. Don't wait until parent-teacher conferences before you mention your daughter can't keep up with her spelling assignments, or your son can't see the chalk board. Regular notes and calls between home and classroom keep communication open, support teachers' efforts and provide a unified educational program for your kids.

6) <u>Get involved in your youngsters' schools</u>. Whether you're a full-time employee or a stay-at-home parent, there are plenty of ways to show your support. Volunteering on the school premises, attending a P.T.A. meeting, donating for a fundraiser and attending the band concert all help out the school and show your kids you value their education.

7) <u>Be available to help your children with their homework</u>. I know this can be a chore when you're tired, or when you have other tots to care for. It can be especially burdensome when your son or daughter repeatedly struggles with nightly assignments. Try to avoid taking on too many evening commitments, or doing so much at home that you can't listen to oral reading or help memorize math facts. Also, never belittle children for asking for help. Let them know with both your words and your attitude that you're always willing to lend a hand.

8) <u>Avoid over scheduling your family</u>. I adhere to the "Two Activity Rule." Each child can be involved in only two extra-curricular activities at one time. The number may vary for your family, depending on the number of children, their ages and your work schedule. It's equally important to keep your own schedule under control. Avoid taking on more than you can manage,

and give yourself lots of permission to say "No," to further demands on your time.

9) <u>Support your children's efforts over their results</u>. Our goal as parents is to help each of our children perform to their highest levels of ability. We want both our gifted kids and our learning disabled youngsters to develop sound study habits and thoughtful, diligent approaches to their work. Praise daughter Shelly's willingness to finish her difficult history questions, even though her grade is a low C. And support Aaron's enthusiastic research for a project he could have aced without opening a book.

10) <u>Celebrate your children's school successes</u>. And I don't just mean the A's. Cheer the note from the teacher commending Marci on her ability to get along on the playground. Rave about son Raul's number of sit-ups in P.E. You'll not only be joining in their victories, but you'll be giving them the message, "I care how you're doing in school." Your wholehearted love and support are the best tools they bring to class.

You Can Improve Your Child's Education

It's popular to criticize schools whenever problems arise with kids. Poor reading scores, low self-esteem and lack of enrichment for top achievers are all fodder for the cannon continually aimed at public education.

But schools may not be the real culprit. In an article appearing in the January 26, 1994 issue of *Education Week,* P. Kenneth Komoski cites an enlightening statistic: In the course of a year, children spend only 19% of their potential learning time in school. A full 81% of our youngsters' time is taken up in non-curricular events at home, daycare, organizations or in free, unstructured activities.

Rather than denouncing the area that influences their kids less than one-fifth of their total time, parents ought to be focusing on improving the way their children use the other four-fifths of their lives. Instead of harping on what is commonly perceived as the "19% problem," efforts would be better served enhancing what Mr. Komoski terms the "81% solution."

I'm certainly not absolving educational institutions from their responsibilities in teaching and positively influencing children. But realizing the limited roles schools play in our kids' days, places the real burden of raising our offspring where it belongs--with the parents.

What can parents do to enhance their children's lives? Plenty! Start by controlling the most common out-of-school activity--television watching and video-game playing. According to Mr. Komoski, kids spend a whopping 25% of their spare time in front of the tube. That's more time than they spend all year in school! Severely curtailing (or even eliminating) TV and video exposure is one sure-fire way to improve your kids' education.

I often hear parents complain their children's schools aren't challenging enough for them. My response is that it is primarily the parents' responsibilities to provide the necessary extra-curricular activities.

For example, family travel offers a cornucopia of learning experiences. You can foster social interaction as you plan and pack for trips. Children can gain map-reading skills and geographical knowledge. They can learn about different cultures, periods of time and languages. They even gain valuable lessons in responsibility, both for themselves and for other members of the family.

If trips aren't in your budget or time-frame, family outings are great, too. Museums, concerts, local historical or cultural sites, and natural phenomena are terrific supplements to class time. Many are even free of cost and augmented by knowledgeable guides or docents.

Find worthwhile after-school organizations or activities for your youngsters to participate in. Brownies, church youth groups, sports and Camp Fire not only provide top-notch programs for youth, but expose children to concerned adults who can double as good role models.

Play games with your kids. Puzzles and board games are some of life's true bargains. They give hours of enjoyment. And they offer lessons in sportsmanship, following rules, strategies and togetherness.

We've even invented our own games. Our most recent involves finding a word in the dictionary, for instance "mule", then asking the other person to think of the word on the same page as "mule" that means "a quick bread baked in a small, cup-shaped mold." Answer: "muffin."

Encourage family projects around the house. Tending a vegetable garden, baking bread, working with wood, repairing the car and pruning trees can foster feelings of togetherness and pride while teaching children life skills. For instance, my son proudly shared with his third grade class that he had built a desk for his room with his father.

When it comes to enriching kids' lives, the possibilities are endless. By recognizing our roles in our children's educations, we are well on our way to finding that "81% solution."

School Work
Helping Your Youngsters Do Their Best

School bells are ringing and it's time for kids to hit the books. But, as children start memorizing math facts and writing book reports, parents need to create home environments that ensure academic success.

Parents begin this process with their attitudes towards their kids' educations. Families who give school work top priority and who make homework their children's "jobs," provide clear messages about their expectations of their youngsters' performances. Those moms and dads who can't find time to help on school projects or listen to first-graders learning to read, convey the message, "School isn't important."

This isn't to say that straight-A's are required. Instead, your child's best effort is the ultimate goal. For some boys and girls, tops grades are achievable. For others, success can't be measured by a G.P.A. Helping students establish appropriate goals boosters both self-esteem and academic success.

Reward effort more than outcome. Much of education involves learning to tackle and complete assignments, handle challenges and follow through with responsibilities. Statements such as, "You really worked hard on that report," or "I know learning those multiplication tables took lots of patience," encourage kids to do their best work, regardless of innate abilities.

Set aside regular times for your youngsters to do homework. This can be somewhat negotiable: some kids may want to get it done as soon as they're home; others may want to play first, then do it before dinner. (Of course, some may prefer not to do it at all, in which case you pick the time for them.)

If they've selected a time, but dawdle or refuse to hit the books, a gentle reminder of their responsibilities will get them back on track. If, after several reminders, they're still having trouble focusing, then use a contingency plan: "You may not play until your assignments are completed satisfactorily. Period."

It's best to have a set place to study. Of course, well-lit desks in the kids' rooms, away from distractions, are optimum. But a kitchen table or counter top can work equally well. Wherever is best, encourage your children to work there regularly. Avoid having them study one night on the sofa, the next night in the bathtub.

Institute a family quiet time--even for those members not studying. Radios and TVs stay off, and everyone reads or entertains themselves silently. This works especially well when kids' ages vary: it tells students, "We value your education," while letting younger tots know, "We'll respect your need for quiet when you're in school."

Keep children's schedules workable so there's plenty of time to complete assignments. This may mean paring down activities during the school year to give homework top priority.

On the other hand, don't necessarily eliminate a favorite pastime because a youngster's struggling in his classes. Sports or special hobbies can provide much needed opportunities for success for less academically oriented children.

Turn Off The TV And Turn On Your Children's Minds

Want to increase your children's intelligence, creativity and motivation? Simple. Turn off the TV.

On the average, children spend 25% of their spare time watching television or playing video games. They watch almost 16 hours of TV every week, but do only three hours of homework during that time. Preschoolers are the largest audience, spending 28 hours (over one full day!) in front of the tube each week.

What's wrong with watching lots of television? Plenty. First off, it's addictive. Television producers specifically design shows that keep little eyes glued to the screen.

In his book, *Four Arguments for the Elimination of Television,* Gerry Mander explains how the use of "technical events" accomplishes this goal: "A technical event is an alteration of the image on the screen by technical means, a change in an image that couldn't possibly happen in ordinary life." Sudden scene changes, cuts from one face to another, moving forward or backward in time...All these interventions serve one purpose--to hold viewer attention.

Mr. Mander goes on to explain that an average TV show has a technical event every six seconds. An expensively produced, prime-time national advertisement can have one every two to three seconds. With all the leaping and flashing taking place on the screen, it's no wonder parents have trouble tearing kids away from the set!

Prolonged exposure to such hyperstimulation decreases children's attention spans. One veteran first-grade teacher told me that, over the course of twenty years, her students have become less able to focus on stories she reads aloud. While they once could listen to 30 minutes of a story without pictures, that time has dwindled to less than ten minutes with numerous pictures.

Television decreases children's creativity and their abilities to entertain themselves. Kids receive external stimulation, rather than relying on their inner resources for diversion.

Finally, television interferes with interpersonal relationships. Ever notice how, when a TV's on in the room, all eyes are upon it? That's because nobody can compete with the hubbub on the tube. Families who watch lots of television usually talk less with each other, and miss out on the richness of each others' lives.

What can you do to break the TV habit in your house?

Start by setting limits. Don't allow kids to simply cruise through the channels, looking for something to do when they're bored. Encourage them to pick one or two favorite shows to watch each week, and keep the set off in between times.

Don't use TV as a baby-sitter. I know, it's a good way to get a few minutes of quiet so you can cook dinner or put your feet up. But using the tube to entertain kids means you'll have kids who are only entertained in front of the tube.

Instead, encourage your children to play by themselves while you do your chores. Provide them with an appropriate play area, then expect them to entertain themselves. Don't cave in to their pleas. You might take a break from your activities every half hour or so to share a story or admire a block house. But letting them know that they can play quietly by themselves helps them develop those skills.

Keep alternative activities available in your home. Puzzles, board games, crafts and good books teach quiet creativity and resourcefulness. Read aloud to your children or, as they get older, listen to them read to you. I enjoy quilting while my sons share their latest books with me.

Set a good example. Don't flop down on the sofa when you are bored. Pick up a good book, or keep an ongoing hobby within easy reach when you want to relax.

Kicking the TV habit may not be easy. But you'll be doing your kids--and yourself--a big favor!

Let's Support Our Public Schools

School-bashing has become a national pastime. Pick up any newspaper, and you'll find an article blasting our public schools. Watch TV for an evening, and you'll hear how far our kids are falling behind. Listen to parents of school-age youngsters, and you'll quickly learn who *not* to request for your child's teacher.

This country's schools are burdened with a Herculean task, namely educating every single boy and girl between the ages of six and 18. Children whose families can't afford pencils, children who will never read because of neurological impairments and children whose parents deal drugs are educated in the same system with children who will become rocket scientists, national leaders and university professors.

Unfortunately, each year kids come to school less prepared to learn. The soaring divorce rates mean that more and more boys and girls are worrying about their parents' fighting instead of learning long division. Rampant unemployment means that youngsters are more concerned about whether Mom and Dad are going to have a job than studying spelling. And increased drug and alcohol use means more kids are wondering if their parents will be stoned, rather than if their parents will attend their soccer games.

Who's responsible for picking up the slack caused by these social problems? Schools, of course. They must now teach drug and alcohol awareness, offer groups for kids going through divorce, provide sexual and moral guidance, educate students about AIDS and steer kids clear of tobacco.

At the same time, funds for education have been slashed. Schools are squeezed to handle more with less.

It's enough to make you want to cancel the school year.

But I'm not writing this to expound on the schools' woes. I'm writing this to enlist your help. We all benefit from the public school system. It's up to all of us to help it out.

Start by supporting your children's schools. Schools are only as strong as the parents who support them. Instead of running the school down, donate your time, cash and enthusiasm.

Your kids will pick up on your attitude. If you are supportive of the school, they're more apt to be respectful to school personnel and classmates.

Know and support your school staff. You're all committed to providing a great educational experience for your children. Work together as a team.

Don't hover over your children. Let them make decisions, deal with problems and generally handle as much of their lives as they can. Your goal is to train them to be completely independent of you. Hovering seriously impairs that development.

Don't fret if every teacher your youngster encounters during her schooling isn't "Teacher of the Year" material. All instructors have their strengths and weaknesses. And even the least inspirational in the profession can teach your kids to get along with various types of people. As in life, the good comes along with the mediocre.

Make school work a priority. School is your kid's job. Giving it full attention will make learning easier for your child and all of his classmates. This may mean limiting extra-curricular activities to ensure there's time and energy for homework.

Show an interest in what's happening in your youngsters' classrooms. Social studies or science topics make great dinner conversations. And encouraging your children to tell you about their days not only helps their verbal and organizational skills, but gives the overwhelming message: "We care about your school."

Parent-Teacher Conferences
Making Them Work For You and Your Child

School conferences are upon us. Throughout the country, parents are approaching their children's teachers to ask the ultimate question, "How is Junior doing?"

I've asked some of this area's most experienced teachers and administrators for their tips on how parents can gain the most from their parent-teacher conferences. Here's what they suggest:

*Be on time. Twenty minutes is barely enough time to cover three months' worth of progress and concerns. Arriving a little early means you'll be physically and mentally ready to make the most of every minute. Arrange for childcare for younger siblings who may be distracting. And don't try to engage the teacher in a lengthy philosophical discussion requiring more than the allotted time. Keep to the topic of your child, so both of you can stay on track.

* Be prepared. Think ahead about what questions or issues you want to cover. Bring in samples of assignments or reading material to discuss. You'll find most teachers have done their homework--parents can help by doing theirs.

* Be specific. Asking an open-ended question, such as, "How's Sara getting along?" is apt to elicit an equally open-ended answer, "Fine." Instead, ask about specific concerns you may be having for your child:

"Tim has had trouble learning to tell time. Have you noticed that, too?" Not only will you lead teachers in a relevant direction, but you'll also cue them in about what to watch for throughout the year.

* Don't wait until the conference to discuss serious problems. There simply isn't enough time. Instead, alert the teacher that Carrie isn't able to complete her homework because it's too difficult as soon as you notice the problem. This situation needs to be nipped in the bud early with regular phone calls, notes and meetings.

* Ask about ways you can help your children at home. Whether your son needs special assistance, or your daughter is breezing through the school year, you can do plenty to enhance their educations. Perhaps you can spend extra time studying geography. Or take trips to the local library. You'll not only be helping them in school, you'll be conveying the message, "Homework is a top priority for me."

* Participate in your child's school experience. Teachers can't help but catch the enthusiasm of supportive parents. Whether you're working in the classroom, visiting with teachers or attending school functions, you'll be showing your youngsters--and their teachers--you care.

* Remember that you, the teachers and your kids are a team working together for the benefit of your children's education. Assisting in whatever ways you have available will insure all three of you have a great year.

Reading Aloud To Your Children
The Best Twenty Minutes of Your Day

The latest publication from the U.S. Department of Education states that reading aloud to your children is the single most important activity for ensuring youngsters' success in school.

Reading aloud to your children enriches their lives in so many different ways. For example, it builds their intelligence. They gain knowledge as they hear about historical or scientific facts. They improve their linguistic capabilities as they're exposed to new words or phrases. They expand their levels of concentration by focusing for extended periods of time on the story. They broaden their imaginative powers by mentally picturing the book's characters, places and events.

Reading aloud to youngsters introduces them to great literature. Tiny tots can follow the simple story lines of Margaret Wise Brown or giggle over the antics of poet Shel Silverstein. Older kids will enjoy Roald Dahl, Mark Twain or E.B. White. By reading the stories to them, you're exposing them to books they enjoy hearing, but aren't yet old enough to read themselves.

Reading aloud to young children helps ready them for school. Kids exposed to books early in their lives learn to read easier than their less experienced classmates. They have stronger verbal skills, as well as a greater appreciation for books and learning.

Reading aloud to your children strengthens your relationship with them. Because reading together requires close, physical contact, an absence of distractions, shared experiences and mutual enjoyment, the result is warm, positive feelings for both parent and child.

Reading aloud to children can be used to calm youngsters who are upset or who have difficulties quieting themselves. Gathering my young sons in my lap, taking out their favorite stories and reading to them in my quietest voice, was a sure-fire method of soothing over their mishaps.

Reading aloud to children can also be relaxing for parents. Many moms and dads find that curling up with their youngsters on a pillow after work and reading a story helps them unwind from the stresses of their days.

How much reading is the right amount? Author Rosemary Wells, in a recent speech to the American Booksellers Association Convention in Los Angeles, recommends parents read to their youngsters twenty minutes daily. Her campaign, "Read Twenty To Your Bunny," encourages parents to make those "the best twenty minutes of your day."

It's never too early to start reading to your kids. Provide your baby with lots of sturdy cloth or cardboard books, and look at them often together. If they're too young to follow a story, look at the pictures, or make up a simpler, abbreviated version of the text.

Take your tots on outings to the library. Help them select enticing picture books. When they're old enough, let them get their own library cards. You'll not only be exposing them to a source of infinite knowledge and enjoyment, you'll be instilling a lifelong appreciation of this invaluable public resource.

Discuss the stories you read with your children and encourage their responses. Ask your toddler, "Elisha, where is the puppy hiding?" Inquire of your preschooler, "Why do you think Grandma is happy in this picture?" Or ask a grade-schooler, "How else could Maggie have solved the problem with her brother?"

Allow your children to select books that interest them. You'll be helping them formulate their own opinions, as well as guaranteeing that you're reading what they like.

Don't be surprised if your toddlers like to hear the same stories over and over again. At certain stages of their lives, very young children crave the continuity of oft-repeated tales. Read them whenever they're requested. This stage won't last forever.

Finally, don't stop reading to your children when they learn to read themselves. Kids still crave the close parental contact and the warm, comforting feelings they get from hearing stories. Let them tell you when they've outgrown it. Until then, sit back, curl up with your kids, and enjoy another book together.

Helping Kids Establish Sound Homework Habits

An article by Dr. Linda Sanna, appearing in the *P.T.A. Monthly Magazine*, offers parents good advice on how to help their youngsters do homework. Her suggestions have been adapted by Laguna Middle School in San Luis Obispo, California, as a part of their Productive Parent Involvement Study Program.

Dr. Sanna believes many parents spend too much time drilling their children on the three R's, and not enough time establishing good study skills. She explains that being able to organize and budget time wisely, handle responsibility and solve problems constructively is as important as algebra, French, reading or social studies.

How can you foster these skills?

1) <u>Start a formal study program at home</u>. Rather than debating whether your son or daughter has homework each evening, simply set aside a regular time for studying or reading. Allow approximately 15 minutes per academic subject per night, or approximately 1 to 1-1/2 hours nightly.

Hold a family meeting and decide with your family which time works best for everyone. Set a specific time and stick with it.

2) <u>Turn off the television, video game and stereo, and unplug the phone for the duration of the study time</u>. This practice not only helps students focus on their school work, but sends a strong message from other

family members: "Your education is important to us. We want you to do your best in school." It even helps soon-to-be-school-aged children get into the nightly study mode.

3) <u>Choose a central location (perhaps in the kitchen or at the dining table) for children to do their studying</u>. Dr. Sanna suggests that it may be wise to reverse the practice of sending kids to their rooms to do their homework. Busy parents and children often have little time to spend together. And those youngsters needing assistance can get help quicker with Mom or Dad nearby.

4) <u>Parents, be available during the entire study time</u>. You may read or pay bills at the study table. Or you may finish cooking dinner or cleaning the kitchen. Whatever you do, stay close to monitor your child's progress and behavior. Dr. Sanna encourages such parental supervision until the study habit is engrained, and the student is mature enough to do homework without guidance.

5) <u>Don't argue with your children about homework</u>. Simply set and enforce a regular study time. You can't make your youngsters do homework, but you can offer them only two options: to study or to sit and stare.

6) <u>Keep an upbeat attitude</u>. Homework isn't meant to be punishment. It's merely preparing your son or daughter to become self-disciplined and to master skills needed in adulthood.

7) <u>Help your children with difficult assignments, but never do their work for them</u>. Assist them in developing the strategies for tackling their own work. Ask, "Josh, where do you think you could find that

answer in your science book?" If he doesn't know where to look, ask more questions that encourage him to think. For example, you might say, "Let's see, it sounds like your question is about insect behavior. Where have you read about that subject in this chapter?"

8) <u>Parents, keep your evenings as free from distractions as possible to ensure your availability to assist your children.</u> I know this is tough. We all lead busy lives. And dinner time can be the roughest time of the day. But our kids' school work must be our family's top priority. And we can't help them if we're too busy, tired or distracted.

This is especially important when kids are having trouble with their school work. Marcos, who was struggling with his vocabulary, needed nightly practice to master his new words. But his father often worked late at night, and his mother was distracted in the evenings by his younger sisters.

When his parents realized how important their involvement was to Marcos' school success, they set aside time right after school to assist him with his words. Their commitment not only helped Marcos' grades, but the time they spent involved with him boosted his self-esteem as well.

Chapter 7

•

Challenging Children

"In the difficult are the friendly forces, the hands that work on us."

Rainer Maria Rilke
185-1926

Managing Your Difficult-To-Like Child

"Help! I don't like my child!" wailed Joni, a competent, caring mother of three active grade-schoolers. "Sure, I love all of my children. But Matthew drives me up the wall. Sometimes I just can't stand him."

Joni is not alone in her struggles with a difficult-to-like youngster. Sometimes parents' personalities clash with their kids' temperaments. For instance, outgoing Dave dearly loved his daughter, Sabrina. But he had trouble relating to her shy, anxious personality. And athletic MarySue adored nine year-old Karl. But she was bewildered by his total resistance to sports.

Other parents dislike their children during particular stages the kids go through. Sherry and daughter Pamela got along fine until Pamela turned twelve. Then Pamela became sullen, demanding, self-centered and generally unpleasant. Sherry didn't like being with her daughter, and was secretly relieved when she left for school each day.

Still other children are just plain difficult to be around. Their personalities are such that almost everyone they encounter finds them challenging.

Whatever the reason, the outcome is the same. Caring, loving parents dislike being with their children, then feel guilty about the way they feel. Not only are their youngsters still unpleasant, but they feel incompetent in their roles as parents, and they feel disloyal to their kids.

What can you do during those times you don't like your children? Start by letting go of your guilt and shame. These feelings don't prove you're a bad parent. Rather, they're an indication that you're human, and that your youngster is being particularly trying. Recognize it as a phase, not a litmus test of your parental abilities.

Look for positive characteristics in your child. Even the most challenging youngster has some. For instance, Ward couldn't stand daughter Angie's dirty room and slovenly habits. But he acknowledged the fact that her grades were good, and that he could always trust her to be where she said she would be.

Marilyn struggled with five year-old Dylan's non-stop questions. But she realized he was very intelligent, and she appreciated his curiosity about his world.

Find enjoyable activities you can share with your child. For example, Carla was going crazy at home because of two year-old Ben's loud voice and unfocused energy. But she found that taking him to the park was a sheer delight. They could blow bubbles, climb on the structures, feed the birds, and savor each other's company.

Look for someone who appreciates your child's personality, or who shares your child's interests. Anne was high-strung and meticulous, and couldn't stand Cody's love of reptiles and amphibians. She found a biology student at the local university who was willing to take her son with him on field trips.

Rugged Charles couldn't relate to his daughter Shilo's pre-occupation with her appearance and love of high fashion. But rather than argue over their divergent interests, he enrolled Shilo in a teen modeling course where she met other girls and women who shared her passion, and who made Shilo feel important.

Take breaks away from your children. You need time away to recharge your batteries and regain your perspective on your situation. You might try activities with your spouse or other adults. Or you may prefer quiet, meditative time to collect your thoughts. Whichever you choose, allow plenty of time to relax and be yourself.

Finally, if you find yourself disliking your children on a daily, never-ending basis, get help. Parenting classes and individual counseling can improve your discipline techniques and communication skills, as well as minimize your life's stresses.

Helping Kids Cope With Their Own Personalties

Children are born with unique personality styles. Some are shy; others are never quiet. Some youngsters are very active, while others could read silently all day long. As parents, we can help our youngsters develop strategies that capitalize on their personal strengths and successfully manage their individual weaknesses.

Here's what I mean. Ten year-old Thomas is meticulous about his school work, but often turns assignments in late because he works too slowly. Thomas' parents first let their son know how proud they were of his conscientious attitude. Then they used a combination of speed games, timed assignments and attention focusing techniques to help him pick up his pace a little bit.

Unfortunately, many parents view their children's personalities and work styles as faults the youngsters need to conquer. "I don't know why you can't just sit still like all the other kids," Lorna scolded her son, Will, who was having trouble paying attention in class. "All you want to do is play ball on the playground."

What these moms and dads fail to realize is that their criticism only alienates their children, driving them away from their best possible sources of help--their families.

In reality, parents can serve as great resources for their kids because they often have the same personality styles. They can share their feelings with their children of what it was like not being picked for a team at recess. They can offer support for the difficulties their children may be having with teachers. They can teach strategies they developed for handling similar situations. And they can serve as role models of ways to overcome personal challenges.

For instance, Donna had similar learning difficulties as her daughter, Aubrey. But rather than criticizing Aubrey's poor grades, Donna shared with her about how she had learned to make work sheets for herself to help her better organize her studies. She let Aubrey know she understood what she was experiencing, then helped her work out a solution.

How can you help your children develop personal strategies?

Start by assuming a positive approach to your youngsters' personalities and learning styles. Such characteristics are as innate as their genders, their eye colors and their skin tones. Avoid making judgments about something your children cannot change.

Enlist your youngsters' help in finding solutions. For example, you might ask your daughter, Melissa, "What do you think you could do to keep from talking so much to your friends in class, and having to stay in during recess?" Encourage her to take responsibility for the situation, rather than you solving it for her.

Guide your children to lay out specific plans for tackling their situations. For instance, if your son is having problems concentrating in his room, you could ask, "Devon, what do you think is the first thing you could change in here that might make it easier to study?" If Devon can't think of anything, you could try,

"I know when I was your age, I couldn't study if my desk was too cluttered. How do you think your desk could be better organized?"

Practice your new strategies with your children. Let's say you and your daughter develop a plan to help her overcome shyness at her piano recital. She will look people in the eyes as she shakes their hands, and say, "Nice to see you," or "Thank you for coming." Then, you role play her recital, with her coming up to you several times and confidently making her statements.

Finally, evaluate the strategies with your children. Ask yourselves, "How effective have these plans been? Have they improved the situations in the ways they were intended?" If yes, your plans have been successful. If not, they can always be reworked.

Personal strategies are not meant to be final cures. Rather, they are one of numerous coping methods children learn as they mature. Fine-tuning such techniques are a life-long process and serve our kids well in every area of their lives.

Facts About A. D. D.

Robby, age nine, has been diagnosed with attention deficit disorder. He has a hard time listening to directions, is easily distracted from doing his school work, is always on the go and is falling further and further behind his classmates.

Attention deficit disorder (A.D.D.), also known as hyperactivity, is found in an estimated 5-15% of all children. Boys are affected ten times more often than girls. The average age of referral to a physician for evaluation is eight years old. But most parents will attest that the child has been overly active and difficult to handle since birth.

Unfortunately, the problem isn't fully recognized until the youngster starts doing poorly in school. But, by this time, his self image may be severely damaged. He is often ridiculed at home for being a "goof off" or yelled at for not doing as he is told. He may have trouble making friends because he pokes them or can't focus on their games. He gets frustrated because he can't do anything right, but his young body can't settle down long enough to complete any of the tasks expected of him.

The parents of such youngsters suffer, too. Nothing they try seems to change their child's behavior, so they often resort to name-calling, spanking and severe punishments. They feel guilty about what they may have said and done to him, but are at their wits' ends about what to do differently. They may resent their son for the attention he takes away from other family members. They may even wish that he hadn't been born.

What can you do if you suspect your child has A.D.D.? Start by getting an evaluation from your pediatrician or a psychologist trained in assessing this disorder. Once you've received a diagnosis of attention deficit disorder, a two-pronged treatment approach will most likely be taken. The first is to use a medication to help him sit still and focus his attention more easily.

The second is to use a reinforcement program to help the child change some of his behaviors. Here's how it works:

Let's say your child is having trouble sitting still at the dinner table. You make an agreement with him: when he sits quietly at the table for ten minutes, he gets an extra story at bedtime. If he sits quietly for another ten minutes at dinner, he gets one more story. Then, set a timer to ring every ten minutes. If he's having trouble making it through the allotted time, shorten it to seven, or even five minutes. The goal is to reward his appropriate behavior, not be angry at him for disobeying. When he has completed the desired behavior, he is rewarded that evening.

Use this same method in conjunction with his teachers at school. Enlist their help in monitoring his behavior (perhaps by noting on a card each time your son completes a desired task), then letting you offer a reward when he comes home.

Adapt the reward to fit your individual child. Your youngster might prefer watching a TV program, playing a game or helping make a favorite meal. One of my sons liked getting back-rubs, so we used those for behavioral rewards. Use the R.O.A.R.S. principle as a guideline: Reward Often And Reward Small. You don't need to offer trips to Disneyland, Nintendo systems or Fast Trax to help your child change his behavior.

Keep a positive attitude when using these techniques. Remember, you're helping your child with a difficult task. He needs your support. Be as enthusiastic and encouraging as you can.

Different Drummers
Helping Unique Youngsters Manage Their Lives

Is your child teased by her classmates?

Does he prefer to play by himself rather than with friends?

Are her interests notably different from other children her own age and gender?

Does he choose to wear clothes that are different from others in his class?

Is she of average or higher than average intelligence, yet finding her school experience unsuccessful?

Does he have a problem fitting in with his peers?

Does she have few, if any, friends?

If yes, then your child may be what I call a "Different Drummer," a child who is repeatedly noted as being different from other classmates, a child whose primary distinction is not fitting in with his or her peers.

Different Drummers are of at least average intelligence, with some possessing high or even superior intellectual capabilities. They are usually devoid of any learning or behavioral abnormalities. In fact, they are seen as capable children in almost every aspect of their lives.

However, Different Drummers can create high levels of stress for their families. Their parents often expend great deals of energy helping them behave like other kids. They may buy them stylish clothing, or invite classmates over for a party. Unfortunately, such efforts usually prove fruitless, causing frustration and anger for the parent, and a sense of failure for the child.

To make matters worse, the mothers and fathers of Different Drummers were often Different Drummers themselves. They regularly report having experienced the pain of being teased on the playground, excluded from birthday parties and called names during recess. Such memories are rekindled as they watch their own youngsters suffer, and often elicit over protection to keep their children from being psychologically hurt.

However, such reactions only compound the problem. Parents hoping to shape children into being "normal" reinforce the notion that their youngsters are different and therefore bad. They discount their personal preferences and styles. And their attempts to replace their sons' and daughters' "unacceptable" tastes leave the kids wearing clothes and doing activities that just don't feel right.

Such well-meaning efforts also isolate the children from their best support systems--their families. Such feelings of abandonment compound their sense of worthlessness, and further decrease their self-esteem.

What can you do if your child is a Different Drummer?

First off, avoid solving your child's problems. He will have to deal with this personality style all of his life. Let him discover how best he can get along.

Listen to your child's concerns. Acknowledge his feelings. Perhaps share a similar incident you experienced. Don't pity him. Simply offer a non-judgmental ear.

Discuss strategies for tackling problems your child brings to you. Let's say someone is calling your daughter names. Together, you think of steps she can take, such as turning away, enlisting the help of a teacher or telling the offender to leave her alone.

Provide your youngster with safe opportunities to interact with other kids. Invite an occasional friend over, or plan to meet someone at the park. Don't expect these to necessarily blossom into lifelong friendships. The goal is to simply improve social skills.

Expose your child to a variety of different people and activities. Perhaps your daughter will discover a new interest that suits her perfectly. Or maybe your son will meet a friend who shares his passion for astronomy.

Focus on your child's strengths. Give him plenty of chances to shine at what he does best.

Finally, accept your child for the unique creation that he is. Your love and unconditional acceptance will be the best help you can give him.

Sensitive Children Need Extra TLC

Does your child cry easily?

Is she moody?

Does he overreact to loud noises or changes in his environment?

Was she a demanding, fussy baby?

Is he allergic to foods, pollens, molds or pets?

Does she become overly dramatic about seemingly minor problems?

Does he have physical complaints, even though nothing is medically wrong?

Is she emotionally demanding and draining to be around?

Then your child may be a Sensitive Child, a tot who experiences and reacts to his or her environment in a more stressful way than other, less sensitive youngsters.

Sensitive Children are highly responsive to physical sensations in their lives. Clothes that feel normal to others may be irritating to their skin. Barely noticeable odors may make them nauseous. Particular sounds may hurt their ears. Baths or swimming pools may be distasteful for them to enter. And aches and pains that go unnoticed by other tots may send Sensitive Children into fits.

Emotional changes and fatigue also challenge Sensitive Children. For example, the excitement of a birthday party may stress a Sensitive Child to tears. Or a missed nap, combined with a visit from grandparents, can elicit tantrums and total loss of emotional control.

Sensitive Children sometimes suffer from allergies to food or environmental pollutants. Milk, wheat or yeast allergies are especially common, as are sensitivities to pets, pollens, dust or household chemicals.

In short, Sensitive Children are youngsters who are physically and psychologically less tolerant of their surroundings than other boys and girls.

Unfortunately, Sensitive Children are often misunderstood by their parents, teachers and classmates, and labelled as neurotic, controlling or demanding children. Rather than being given assistance in coping with their already taxing lives, they are told to "Pull themselves together," "Quit making such a fuss," or "Stop overreacting." Such admonitions only make Sensitive Children feel worse by inducing guilt over situations they cannot control.

What can you do to help Sensitive Children function more successfully in their lives?

Start by recognizing that both their personalities and their physiologies are out of their control. They are coping with their lives as best they can, and they are definitely not looking for attention or intentionally being manipulative.

Minimize the stresses Sensitive Children experience in their days. Sure, some stresses--like school work and chores--are unavoidable. But after-school activities should be kept to a minimum. And celebrations, such as birthday parties, should be small and simple.

Have your child tested for allergies, especially if they run in the family. An allergist can help you learn what to avoid to minimize toxins in your child's system.

Help your child develop strategies for dealing with stressful situations. For example, you can teach your teen-age daughter how to take deep breaths and think calm thoughts to relax herself while taking tests. Or you might gently tell your seven year-old son that he can go to his room and listen to a soothing tape when he feels overloaded.

Parents, if you were also Sensitive Children, share your experiences with your youngsters. Perhaps you developed your own way of coping with the anxiety of the first day of school. Or maybe you can relate to your daughter's fear of not being able to control herself in public. You'll not only be showing your support for what your kids are going through, but you'll be strengthening your emotional bonds with them as well.

Finally, recognize that being a Sensitive Child is your child's personal issue, not yours. You can be caring and supportive. But you can't solve his problem. You'll be most helpful by simply allowing him to discover his own solutions, and by lovingly acknowledging his progress from the sidelines.

Bedwetting
Helping Your Youngster Stay Dry

Uh-oh. Six year-old Jamie wet his bed again last night. His parents are sure he ought to have outgrown this problem by now. But no amount of pleading, threatening or punishing has kept him dry. Mom and Dad are at their wits' ends. Jamie feels embarrassed and ashamed.

Bedwetting, or nocturnal enuresis, is a problem for many children, effecting twice as many boys as girls. It comes in two forms. Primary enuresis, the most common type, refers to children over the age of five who have never been able to stay dry through the night. Secondary enuresis applies to children who were dry for a period of time, but started wetting again, usually as a result of a stressful occurrence or anxiety.

Primary enuresis is usually caused by a delay in the child's physical maturation. While most boys and girls gain complete bladder control by age four or five, approximately 15% of children still wet their beds at night by the time they start school. Three per cent of youngsters continue to wet by age 10, with a few wetting into adolescence.

Bedwetting tends to be genetic. Studies show that night time bedwetters very likely have one or both parents who also wet their beds.

A very recent theory suggests that some night time wetters may be deficient in an antidiuretic hormone, known as vasopressin, which regulates urine flow from the kidney to the bladder. Children who continue wetting past the usual age may be slow to produce this hormone. Giving such youngsters desmopressin, an antidiuretic hormone usually administered as an aerosol nasal spray, is showing promise as a successful treatment.

What can you do if your child wets the bed? First of all, be as calm and understanding as you can be. I know this can be hard. But your child desperately needs your help, not your anger, guilt or humiliation.

Try these simple measures:

*Limit your child's evening fluid intakes. Put away the drinking glass after 7:00 p.m.

*Wake your child before you go to bed, and take him to use the toilet. With older children, you can set an alarm to awaken them and remind them to go.

*Install a nightlight in the rooms of kids who might be afraid of the dark and, therefore, reluctant to get up at night to use the toilet.

*Buy your child a washable sleeping bag. It's easier to toss it in the washing machine than to change all the bed linens.

If these steps don't work, schedule a visit with your pediatrician. Rule out any medical problems, such as infections, diabetes, kidney problems or structural abnormalities.

Set up a system that rewards your child's dry nights. One clever parent told me how she used a dot-to-dot picture which led her son up to a desired toy. Each morning the child awoke dry, he was allowed to connect two more dots. After he reached the desired number, he received his prize.

Alarms can also be effective. These come in the form of small, portable, battery-operated devices worn close to the body that are held in place by underpants. Moisture activates the alarm as soon as the child starts to wet, signalling the child to get up and use the toilet.

Bedwetting alarms have a success rate of 60-80%, and work best on older children who are highly motivated to stay dry, and who are wet more than half of their nights.

Above all, stay supportive and positive with your youngster. Time and patience are your two allies. You want your child to feel as victorious in the process of overcoming bedwetting as you do in the actual dryness itself.

Helping Kids Cope With Nightmares

Four year-old Cassidy awakens, screaming, in her bed. Her parents rush to her room and find her eyes wide open and her face flushed and sweating. When they try to comfort her, she acts as if they aren't in the room, stiffening and pushing them away. No matter what they try, Cassidy doesn't wake up. A few minutes later she collapses back to sleep.

Cassidy was experiencing a night terror, a sleep disturbance most common in children between the ages of three and five, although infants and toddlers may experience them, too.

Night terrors are physiological in origin, and are considered to be variants in a child's normal sleep cycle. They are a result of transitions between the phases of sleep that we all experience every night. First, we fall asleep, then drift into a deep, dreamless stage. A few hours later, we move into a lighter phase of sleep known as rapid eye movement (REM) sleep. Throughout the night, we shift back and forth between deep sleep and REM.

Although adults make this sleep transition with little problem, children with night terrors are experiencing difficulty. They end up half awake and half asleep.

No one's quite sure why youngsters scream and cry during night terrors. But one reason may be that the symptoms of night terror--racing heartbeat and sweating--are associated with panic and fear in the brain. The child appears terrified, although nothing scary has happened.

When children have night terrors, it's best not to interfere. Don't attempt to awaken, comfort or hold them. It's a good idea to stay in the room, though, in case they try to climb out of bed or do something that could hurt themselves.

Night terrors are different from nightmares. Nightmares are emotional in origin, usually caused by some stressful event or fear in the child's life. Unlike night terrors, they can be remembered when the child awakens. And, after a nightmare, a child will very much want to be comforted.

You can help children diminish the fears that trigger nightmares. For example, if your daughter is afraid of monsters, turn the lights on and show her the room is safe. One set of parents I know sprinkled "Monster Dust" (actually glitter) around their child's room to ensure the spooky creatures didn't return.

Encourage children who are old enough to talk to tell you about their nightmares. Listen calmly and attentively. Don't over react to what they tell you. You want them to feel that you are in control.

Never berate children for being frightened during nightmares. Don't accuse them of being babyish or sissies. They are truly petrified and need consolation, not belittling.

Help kids conquer their fears by teaching them how to fight back in their dreams.

Here's how: Let's say your son tells you that a scary man chases him in his dreams and splashes him with water. You tell your son that the next time he sees that man in his sleep, you want him to turn around and scream at him, "GO AWAY! You can't scare me any more!" Your son can even punch him in the nose, then jump on him until he cries for mercy. Your child will have fun scheming about what he'll do and say, and he'll be regaining power over his dreams in the process.

Nightmares can be diminished by regular, calm, soothing nightime rituals. Avoid scary television shows or disciplinary talks at bedtime. Instead, use gentle stories, warm baths, soft songs and pleasant words to create an atmosphere of security.

When Children Pick Friends You Don't Like

Sometimes children pick friends that their parents don't like. For instance, Paul and Maria couldn't stand the girl their son, Mark, was dating. And Barbara thought her daughter's friend, Hannah, was a bad influence on her child.

Many parents respond by forbidding their youngsters to see such friends. But such a tactic is not only ineffective, it may achieve the exact opposite results of those that were intended.

To begin with, you usually don't have control over who your children see when they're not with you. At school, kids can meet at recess, in classes and at school events. Short of keeping your youngsters in isolation, they are on their own much of the time.

Forbidding them to see their friends may even encourage kids to become sneaky and start lying about where they are or whom they're with. When this happens, you've lost even more control of what they're doing.

Such friends obviously fill a need for your children. Your daughter's boyfriend may make her feel special. Or your son's buddies may make him feel as if he belongs. Forbidding your children to see them deprives your youngsters of the benefits they're receiving from their friends.

Such losses may actually push your youngsters further toward the friends you disapprove of. If their friends make them feel wanted, and their parents are critical and disapproving, a closer kinship is likely to develop as the friends face a hostile world together.

This happened with Cynthia and her mother. When Mom forbade Cynthia to see her best friend, Cheryl, Cynthia drew even closer to Cheryl because she understood what Cynthia was experiencing at home.

Finally, children need to learn how to make choices. If we criticize one of their most important decisions, their friends, we give them the message they are poor decision makers, and they are less capable people.

What can you do about the friends of your children you disapprove of? Accept them and welcome them into your home. Invite them over for dinner. Take them to the movies. Include them in your weekend plans. I know, this idea may sound crazy. But embracing your youngsters' companions creates a positive environment for growth for every person involved.

Here's why. Spending time around your children's friends lets you get to know them. You may discover hidden, positive qualities, and come to appreciate what your son or daughter sees in a special buddy.

Including your children's friends in your lives provides the kids with constructive, supervised time to be together. You won't have to worry where your son and his girlfriend are if you've invited them on a family camping trip.

Embracing your children's friends prevents a barrier of resistance and hostility from developing. They can't rebel against your acceptance as easily as they can against your disapproval. And, if at some point, your kids decide they're no longer attracted to particular friends, they won't have to stay together just to prove their parents wrong.

You'll be supporting your children's decisions and teaching them you trust and value their judgments in other people.

You'll be able to offer assistance to your children's friends. Perhaps you're troubled because your daughter's best friend's parents are alcoholics. Rather than excluding the friend, you can listen to her concerns, provide a different role model or support her through the rough times.

Finally, embracing your children's friends keeps communication open for discussing other strategies and concerns. For example, you might say to your son, "I know Justin is a good friend. And I can see why you like him. But I'm concerned about his reckless driving, and I'm worried he'll get in an accident when you're with him. Let's think of some other options to his driving you to the concert this weekend."

When Children Want To Run Away From Home

Neil was six years old when he ran away from home.

Actually, he only had the courage to ride his bike in circles around the driveway for half an hour before he came back in. But he had packed his belongings and had reached the conclusion he could no longer live with us.

The decision had been made an hour earlier. Neil had returned home from kindergarten with a book club form and was excitedly showing me what he wanted to order. Ninja Turtles were the hit at the time, and he had his heart set on a Ninja video being offered through this club. The price was $14.00.

Now, I was not a Ninja Turtles fan. In fact, I downright loathed those little critters. My kids, who watched minimal amounts of television, had been kick boxing and wearing headbands for months. We'd had to enact a rule in our household stating feet had to stay on the floor at all times. Kicking each other in the face was not acceptable. I was not going to pay fourteen dollars to support cartoon characters I had banned from my home.

Neil was very disappointed. He pleaded with me for a few minutes. Then he started to cry. Finally, he grew serious. Looking me squarely in the face, he stated, "If I can't get this video, I'll have to leave this house. I just can't stay here anymore."

It's not unusual for kids to threaten to run away. And I know many parents recommend telling them, "Go! Pack your things. Have a great time."

But I could tell Neil was struggling. He had just made the most frightening decision a youngster can ever make. I didn't feel the need to treat it lightly.

"That must be scary to think of running away," I said.

"N-N-No," he sobbed.

"I'm going to miss you," I told him.

"I'm not going to miss you," he sputtered.

"I think we can find a solution," I suggested.

"No, I can't stay here," he responded. He turned and marched to his room.

Twenty minutes later, he appeared with a small sack of belongings and announced he was leaving. I hugged him, repeating I would be sad without him, and again offering to negotiate. No, he told me. This was it.

I walked him to the door, saw him hop up on his bike, then watched him anxiously from the window while he rode around the driveway. It was only 30 minutes, but it felt like an eternity.

When he returned, I met him at the door.

"I'm glad you're back," I told him. "I missed you. Would you like to come sit with me for awhile?"

We curled up together in a big chair. I spoke softly as we rocked:

"You know, we're a family and we can't just walk away. We all need each other. We have to find solutions to our problems. Is there any way we can solve this one?"

"We don't have any good videos," he whispered. "They're all too babyish. I want to watch something for older kids."

"Sounds like you've outgrown our old videos," I responded. "But I still don't like Ninja Turtles. Are there any other videos you would like that are for older boys?"

He agreed that might be a solution, and I promised to look at videos the next day. In fact, we ended up buying a video about a boy who raced cars. I felt comfortable with our compromise. And I was glad to have Neil home.

Chapter 8

Marriage

"There is no more lovely, friendly and charming relationship, communion or company than a good marriage."

Martin Luther
1483-1546

Successful Marriages
Compromise is the Key

Recently, my husband, Fred, and I were pondering the success of our fifteen-year marriage. Why had we stayed together, while other relationships crumbled around us? Why were many of our friends talking with their attorneys more often than they talked to each other? Or spending more time battling over their children's custody than watching them play soccer?

As usual, Fred had the answer: Looking me straight in the eye, and with the honesty of a saint, he explained, "Because I do everything your way."

I was flabbergasted! Here, for the last decade and a half, I thought I had done everything *his* way!

After the dust settled, and I regained my wits, I realized therein lay the key to our longevity. *Each* of us was willing to give in to the other, to compromise what we wanted for the benefit of the relationship.

In a marriage, stubbornness is not a virtue. Instead, "otherness," flexibility and an ability to give and take are the characteristics keeping couples afloat.

Let me give you an example. Dad doesn't get home from work until 6 p.m., and would like an hour to unwind before dinner. But the rest of the clan is starving, with homework and bathtime clammoring in the wings. One solution? Dad eats dinner with the family (even if it's not his favorite time) on Mondays and Wednesdays, and, on Tuesdays and Thursdays, they eat without him. He gets time to relax and time to eat with the family. They've reached a workable compromise.

What happens when issues are too important to give in on? Don't panic. Try this little exercise:

Each person involved in the decision rates the importance of the issue on a scale of one to 10, with "one" meaning "of little importance," and "10" being "earth-shattering." Then, compare ratings. The person with the highest rating on the problem gets to run the show, while the other takes a temporary back seat. No fair holding grudges or sabotaging the other's success. This technique only works if both of you are willing to sometimes give in.

Here's what I mean: You're selecting a pre-school for your daughter, and you can't reach an agreement. You want the one close to home so you can carpool, but your spouse has heard good things about the one across town. Whenever you bring up the matter, you both argue about who cares most for your child, avoiding making a decision and creating hurt feelings.

When you compare the decision's relative importance, you score it a "nine," while your husband only rates it a "five." Because you have more emotionally invested in the decision, you get to make the choice--this time. (Note: This technique won't work if one partner rates every decision a "10." Honesty is imperative in deciding what really matters.)

When an issue comes along that you both rate "10," then alternate who's in charge. If, for example, you're remodeling your house, and you both have definite opinions, let one of you take care of the colors and fabrics, while the other looks after design and construction. You'll each have equal input, and your marriage will remain intact.

Managing Long-Distance Marriages

Cliff works out of the area during the week, and is home from Friday evening to Sunday. He is eager to see his wife, Donna, and their two sons, ages four and two. But the lengthy separations are taking their toll. Cliff and Donna don't want to spend their brief time together arguing, but are at a loss as to how to manage their weekend marriage.

All relationships, whether close-contact or long-distance, must balance each participant's needs. Individuals require time to meet personal needs, time to tend to chores and responsibilities, family time with children, and adult time with the other partner.

Balancing these requirements challenges all relationships. But the task becomes even more complex for long-distance relationships. Such couples must still meet everyone's needs, but within a very compact framework. They operate as a micro-marriage, condensing all facets into two days a week.

The job may seem overwhelming. But with awareness and sensitivity, constructive communication, negotiation and careful scheduling, solutions can be reached.

In our family cited above, Cliff is tired when he first gets home Friday night, and needs time to himself. Donna, who is burned-out after being a single parent of pre-schoolers for five days straight, must learn not to over burden Cliff with immediate childcare and household duties. The boys must also give Daddy a few minutes to himself before begging him to come and wrestle with them.

Cliff and Donna agreed that he would get an hour of undisturbed time Friday night before anyone would bombard him. He uses that time to read his mail, unpack his clothes and read the evening paper. Then, he plays with his kids while Donna cooks dinner.

The couple then negotiated that, after dinner, Cliff would bathe the boys, read them a story and put them to bed. Dad could see his youngsters and Mom could take a break. Both parents are adamant about an early bedtime for the kids. They have set aside Friday nights for themselves.

Saturday morning is chore time. Cliff mows the lawn and tends to the cars. Donna does laundry and works in the garden. Saturday afternoon is scheduled for flexible free time. Sometimes Cliff watches the children while Donna runs errands; at other times he goes off surfing with his buddies.

The family spends Sunday morning together before Cliff packs up to get ready for work.

At first, Cliff and Donna resisted scheduling their time so carefully. They longed for the spontaneity they had felt when they were newly married, and when he worked closer to home. But the couple realized that they couldn't rely on chance to meet all of their needs. It was better to consciously decide where to expend their precious moments than to feel bitter and frustrated when needs were overlooked.

Cliff and Donna also had to work hard at learning how to effectively communicate in their long-distance marriage. They needed to identify and solve problems in their relationship, rather than ignore them and let them fester. Cliff made a special effort to understand Donna's struggles with the children. Donna tried to avoid dumping all her stresses on her husband.

Donna realized that she could not expect her husband to spend all weekend relieving her of childcare responsibilities. She had to find support for herself during the week. Because finances were limited, she joined a baby-sitting cooperative so that she could trade baby-sitting time with other families.

An Important Note To Mothers
"Don't Forget Your Husband"

Maureen is a perfect mom. She serves as president on the pre-school board, buys intellectually stimulating toys for her children, and keeps a house that passes white-glove inspection. But Maureen is overlooking one important item--her husband.

Mothers can get so involved in caring for their small youngsters and babies that Dad becomes the Invisible Man. He assumes the role of paycheck and off-duty sitter. But he's left out of his primary job as marital partner.

It's easy to see why this happens. Young tots' demands on their mothers are never ceasing. And the house needs constant effort to avoid looking like post-disaster clean-up. To top it all off, most new moms are perennially pooped. The needs of a spouse are the furthest things from their minds.

Unfortunately, little notice is given to the fact that a father's life is disrupted by children, too. Financial burdens increase with each arrival, and are heightened by the likely reduction of the wife's income.

The home front is turned topsy turvy; once peaceful evenings are now filled with crying, bickering and bath time. Childcare duties may start as soon as he walks in the door, allowing little time to unwind from work. And the emotional support once enjoyed from his spouse has now been rudely replaced by such statements as, "Can you please get a towel. She's spit up again."

Moms, you can draw your mate back into the family by first recognizing he has needs, too. This is not to say one parent's role is more demanding than the other's. Rather, it's to acknowledge that each of you is experiencing parental stresses. You both need to pull together.

Arrange off-duty time for both of you. Dad, maybe you can watch the kids on Thursday afternoon so Mom can ride her bike. Mom, how about giving Dad one night off each week so he can play softball with his buddies?

Set limits on your commitments. Don't use all your energy on committees at church, the pre-school or in the community. You only have a finite amount of energy. Save some of it for your partner.

Establish priorities for your time. List ten items to which you'll devote your resources. Then give yourself permission to not do anything else.

Set aside "Adults Only" time in the evening to chat, snuggle and simply be together. I know this can be hard. But it's vital to keeping the two of you connected.

To make sure you can keep your eyes open past 8:30 at night, try putting your feet up for fifteen minutes in the afternoon so you're not so exhausted after dinner. Dad, maybe you can bring home a take-out dinner so Mom can have more time to re-charge.

If evenings are out of the question, be creative about finding other time to be together. Maybe you can join each other for lunch while Junior's still at pre-school. Or perhaps you can get up a little earlier in the mornings so you have a few moments to catch up on each others' days. My husband and I find exercising together before the children are up is a good way to share and keep in touch.

Make use of sitters. You can even hire someone on a regular basis so you can establish a regular "Date Night" with your spouse.

Don't let tight finances get in the way. How about swapping childcare duties with a friend whose youngsters are the same age? Or putting Baby in the stroller for his nap while the two of you cruise the mall?

One creative couple I know hired a sitter for one hour every Wednesday night so they could dash over to their favorite Mexican restaurant. They each drank a 50 cent beer, ate their fill of complimentary chips and salsa, then raced home to relieve the sitter. The total cost was under five dollars, but the value to their relationship was immeasurable.

Chapter 9

Divorce And Blended Families

"Healing is a matter of time, but it is sometimes also a matter of opportunity."

Hippocrates
c. 460-400 B. C.

Divorce
Minimizing its Impact on Your Children

According to the American Psychiatric Association, divorce is a severely stressful event for the children involved.

While you can't shield your kids from the effects of your break up, you can take steps to make the transition go as smoothly as possible.

Maintain a positive relationship with your former spouse. Even though you are no longer living together, you must still communicate frequently about the welfare of your children.

If you're having trouble being civil to each other, or if your talks regularly degenerate into quarrels, follow these guidelines:

* Decide on one topic to discuss, then stick to it. Don't let yourselves get side-tracked into pointless bickering.

* Be polite. The first snide remark will probably pull the plug on your conversation, so go out of your way to be nice.

* Look for specific solutions to your problems. Are you trying to find good childcare? Do you need to get tutoring for your daughter? Try to find the best answers, and avoid rehashing your relationship.

* Get help if you just can't seem to communicate. A trained counselor will help you direct your energies and make progress.

Never downgrade your spouse in front of your children. I know it's hard. But you are the one having difficulty with the person, not your kids.

The first and strongest lessons youngsters get about how to be a man and a woman, and a mother and a father, are from their parents. Telling your son, "All men are worthless. Just look at your dad," not only makes him feel bad about his father, but gives him distorted, negative messages about who he will be when he grows up.

Don't expect your former husband or wife to parent the same way you do. You can't regulate the kind of television programs the kids watch or the kind of food they eat when they are with the other partner.

All you can do is negotiate as best you can about the important problems, such as which school to attend, then let go of those issues over which you have no control.

Make as few changes as possible in your children's lives. Changes are stressful, and a child going through a divorce is already feeling anxious. Try to minimize other changes by keeping your youngsters with the same baby-sitter, at the same school, and with the same piano teacher.

Structure is comforting, so try to maintain a regulated environment. For example, pick children up from daycare at regular times and assign routine household chores to older boys and girls. You'll find that daily patterns develop kids' security and minimize their anxiety.

Listen to your youngsters and be supportive of their feelings, but don't tolerate rude or abusive behavior.

Help them direct their anger constructively through art, sports, a punching bag or an old stuffed toy they can call names. Many schools offer groups for children experiencing a divorce. Ask your child's teacher or guidance counselor for more information.

Finally, make sure that you, the parent, are getting your personal needs met. It's easy to feel overwhelmed by the kids' demands and overlook your own. You may also be feeling guilty and responsible for your children's pain.

Give yourself permission to heal. Don't over commit yourself. Say "No," to all unnecessary demands on your time.

Find time to recharge your batteries. Take walks, go out with friends or curl up with a good book. After all, helping yourself is one of the best ways you can help your kids.

Blending Families Together
A Formidable, Yet Workable, Task

Al and Peggy would like soon to be married. But the thought of combining all their children from previous marriages is causing them to wonder if their new marriage can succeed.

Millions of couples are faced with the challenge of blending several families into one. And, while the new arrangement can ultimately evolve into a functional unit, it is not usually arrived at without great effort from all involved.

For one thing, children are often reluctant participants in their new domestic situations. While the adults approach their romances optimistically, as a chance to get their lives back on track after a divorce, the kids may view that same change with disdain.

They may resent all the adaptations foisted upon them by their parents' break up. They didn't choose to move to a new house, to enroll in a new school, or to have to try out for a new volleyball team.

The arrival of a new step-mom or step-dad only adds fuel to their hostility. Trying to live under the same roof with such resentment can test the patience of the most saintly spouse-to-be.

Then there's the question of who's really in charge. Does Dad preside over his kids, while Mom keeps tabs on hers? And what about all the ex's? Blended families can have so many variables, it seems impossible to keep them all straight.

But don't give up. There are definite tactics you can use to successfully blend families together.

Start by taking control. Mom and Dad, you are now in charge. No matter how long you've been together, or how much flak you're getting from ex's and kids, you must pull together as a team and make joint decisions. The sooner you act as a unit, the sooner things will fall into place.

Decide together how to handle each situation. Avoid making one member of the couple feel powerless. Each of you has equal say.

For example, if you, Mom, don't like his two year old, figure out together how best to solve the problem. And Dad, don't negotiate alone with your ex-wife about your children. Involve your new spouse as an equal partner in the process.

Create new rules for your family. Establish how things will go in *this* household, not how they went before. Statements such as, "I know you can watch more television at your dad's house. But here it stays off until the weekend," provide structure and clear guidelines about expected behavior.

Hold family negotiating meetings. Give the kids say about how responsibilities will be divided, or how living arrangements can best be worked out.

All children have equal say in the new family. Don't allow his three teenagers to overpower your seven year-old. Rules and policies must cover all youngsters, regardless of their original families.

Recognize that children may be angry, but never tolerate rude or abusive behavior. Set clear limits on what can and can't be done, and provide outlets for dealing with hostility.

Blended families may have irregular visits from its members. For instance, Dad's daughters may only visit every other weekend, and Mom's two children may be gone every summer. Such situations are the norm in blended families and should be included in the plans.

For instance, you may give ten year-old Kate the pet feeding chores when she visits during the Holidays. Or provide Pierre and Jonas with their own room when they live with you during alternate weeks.

Finally, be patient. Just as biological families have the advantage of growing from the pregnancy clear through the teen years, blended families must also gradually mature. Don't expect immediate results.

Managing Your Ex-Spouse's New Relationship

Margie has been divorced from Dave for two years. But, since they live in the same community, and are both actively involved in their young daughter Krissy's life, Margie often finds herself in the uncomfortable position of seeing Dave and his new girlfriend at dance recitals and school plays.

For the most part, Margie has adapted well to her divorce from Krissy's father. She has embarked on a career she enjoys, purchased a new condominium of her own and settled into her role as a single parent.

However, seeing Dave with Adrianne, a woman he began dating before their divorce was final, rekindles many of the unpleasant memories Margie has worked so hard to leave behind. She finds herself struggling with feelings of inadequacy and failure. "If I had been prettier and more intelligent, this wouldn't have happened," Margie tells herself when she sees them. "I failed at being a wife."

Margie appreciates the fact that Dave wants to share responsibilities for raising their child. She realizes how much Krissy loves her dad, and how eagerly she awaits their weekly outings. She also knows it is time to move forward in establishing a new and separate life. Still, she dreads having to face him with his girlfriend.

What can she do to get a handle on the situation? She can start by recognizing there will be no clear-cut answer to her dilemma. No solution will completely alleviate her discomfort. Her goal should be simply to establish a workable, functioning relationship with Dave and Adrianne that allows all parties to successfully share in Krissy's life.

She must remind herself of the benefits of joint custody for Krissy's development, and be grateful Dave wants to be involved. She needs to set aside her anger and hurt feelings for the well-being of her daughter. This won't automatically soothe over years of bitterness, of course. But it will help Margie set her sights on what is most important to her.

Margie will want to control her negative self-talk. Currently, whenever she sees Dave, her mind triggers an inner dialogue of negative statements. She tells herself, "I'm so inadequate and unattractive. I could never be the person he deserved. Look how quickly he found someone to replace me." Then she feels thoroughly depressed and miserable.

Instead, Margie can replace those destructive messages with positive, constructive ones. For instance, reminding herself, "I've made some major changes in my life. I've never felt stronger or more capable," not only boosts her morale, but prepares her to confidently face her former spouse.

She must avoid getting discouraged when old, derogatory self-talk slips back in. She's had lots of practice at those old messages. Gently confessing, "Hey, I'm not perfect. These slip-ups just prove I have room for even more progress," restores her positive attitude, and keeps her feeling competent and calm.

Problem-solving will be in order. She must ask herself, "What would make this situation work better?

Should we sit apart at school events? Or should we sit together? Should we greet each other cordially? Should we not look at each other?" Margie can brainstorm possible solutions, then take constructive steps to implement the new plans. Remember, no solution will be a cure-all. The goal is to simply establish a functional relationship.

Margie must find support from others around her to build her self-esteem. Most parents get down on themselves after their marriages break up. Therefore, it's imperative to create a network of caring, understanding and sympathetic associates to listen to concerns, and help reconstruct tattered egos. Co-workers, organized groups such as Parents Without Partners, neighbors, family members or parents of children's friends are all possible sources. Whoever they are, Margie will need to turn to them for suggestions and emotional nurturing. They are crucial to every divorced parent's well-being.

Finally, Margie must realize that healing from a divorce is an ongoing process. It does not happen overnight. Allowing her progress to proceed at its own pace will let Margie's new life unfold, and let her secure an ever stronger relationship with her daughter.

Dispelling Myths About Divorce

As a marriage counselor, I see many husbands and wives who are considering divorce. They are struggling in their relationships, and are desperately searching for answers.

Unfortunately, divorce isn't a one-step solution. In fact, when young children are involved, separation may create as many new problems as it solves.

Below are three common issues that are often overlooked by warring parents:

<u>Your relationship with your spouse doesn't end when you get divorced</u>. A divorce ends your marriage. But, if you have children, you must maintain a workable relationship with your former partner. Sure, you may be seething with rage. And you may not want to ever see that person again. However, you're still going to have to hammer out your youngsters' living arrangements, homework policies and vacation schedules on a regular basis.

This fact caught Jan by surprise. She assumed that, when she divorced Paul, her problems with him would be over. She dreamed of being free of his verbal tirades, and of taking charge of her new life.

But their poor communication patterns only transferred into the joint custody negotiations regarding their two toddlers. Jan realized she was spending more energy communicating with him after the divorce than she ever did when they were married.

<u>You will have little control over what happens to your children when they are at your former partner's home</u>. I hear many frustrated, divorced parents issuing similar complaints: "How can I get my ex-husband to help our son with his homework when he stays there during the week?" or "My wife treats our daughters like little babies when they're with her. At my house, they get themselves dressed, fed and off to school without assistance. At her house, she waits on them hand and foot."

The fact is, parents have little or no say about what goes on when the kids are at the other parent's house. Unless a situation is abusive, divorced moms and dads can raise their children as they wish when the youngsters are with them.

This realization was shocking for Stan. He was an avid church-goer, and had emphasized the importance of worship in his home. But, since he and Carline had separated, their four girls were receiving no spiritual training when they were with her. Carline had even stopped going to church. Stan was appalled at this development, yet was powerless to make any changes.

<u>People you don't know, or don't approve of, will be helping raise your children</u>. Once you and your mate have divorced, you have no say over whom your ex-spouse chooses to associate with. He or she may quickly remarry, or jump from relationship to relationship. In either case, the new partners will interact with your children and influence their views of the world.

Claire and Steve had been divorced two years when Steve remarried Elaine. Elaine had a grown child by a previous marriage, and wanted little to do with Steve's fifth-grade son, Brady. Steve and Brady had always been close. But Elaine now refused to allow the boy to accompany them on outings, and encouraged Steve to send him away to camps for lengthy periods during each summer.

Claire felt bad for Brady whenever he visited his dad. Yet she realized she had nothing to say about Steve's life. And Brady still idolized his father. Claire couldn't change the fact that Elaine was now in the picture, and that Brady and Steve would never again be as close.

These three observations about divorce are not meant to dissuade all couples from divorcing. Clearly, some parents and families have greatly benefited by the terminations of the marriages.

Rather, I encourage husbands and wives considering separation to be aware of the issues they are likely to face, and make sure they have exhausted all available options.

Chapter 10

From Pregnancy To Pre-School

"A baby is an inestimable blessing and bother."

Mark Twain
1835-1910

Deciding If You Want To Have Children

George and Wendy have been married five years. Both have good jobs, and they own a modest home. They seem to have it all. Yet they're plagued by a gnawing question: should they have a child?

Their feelings about it waver. Sometimes Wendy is positive she wants to start a family, but then wonders about her suitability to be a parent. Her mother was an alcoholic, and Wendy vowed she would *never* treat her kids the way her mother treated her. She also likes her career as a nurse, and is not sure she wants to set it aside.

George is more concerned about the financial commitment of a family. He earns a good salary as a painting contractor. But he wants to provide his children with the best of everything, and wonders if he'll be able to do that. He also doesn't want to give up his time with Wendy, or his weekend ski trips with his pals.

While the decision to have a child is indeed a monumental one, many couples confuse the issue with other, irrelevant concerns. The question is not whether a couple has time to have a child, or whether it will fit career goals or travel plans. It is not even a matter of financial stability. For, although it is important to be able to provide for the needs of a family, the real decision to have children stretches beyond the bank account or date book.

In fact, the question about having a baby revolves around a fundamental drive to raise and be part of a family as a long-range goal.

To help couples assess their feelings about this goal, I recommend two visualization exercises.

Exercise #1: Find a time and location where you won't be interrupted or distracted. Sit comfortably, close your eyes, and listen to your breathing. Let yourself become more and more relaxed with each breath. After a few moments, imagine yourself in the following scenario: You are in your doctor's office, and you have just been told by your doctor that you have a medical condition that has left you unable to parent a child. Imagine how you feel about this news. Spend a few moments completely experiencing your reaction. When you are done, open your eyes.

Exercise #2: Again, find a quiet, comfortable spot where you won't be interrupted or distracted. Allow yourself to relax and focus on your breathing. When you are sufficiently relaxed, imagine the following: Picture yourself ten years from now. See where you are living. Experience what you are doing. Notice who is in your life with you. Now, move ten years further along. Again, see where you are, what you are doing, and who is in your life. Stay with your image for a few moments, then open your eyes.

Analyze your scenarios. How did you feel being told by your doctor that you were infertile? Sad? Disappointed? Determined to adopt? If so, then children are a part of your life's plan. If, on the other hand, you felt relief, then a family is probably not a goal for you.

When you saw yourself in the future, did it include children? Did you picture yourself with a family? Then you probably do want to have children, regardless of the daily hassles you currently feel. If kids weren't a part of your scenario, then give yourself permission to lead a life that doesn't involve a family, in spite of others' opinions.

These exercises may help with your long-range planning, but they may not remove the anxiety many couples still feel at the thought of having children. If this is your case, recognize that you're not alone in your trepidations; many couples dread the unknowns of having babies. Still, it's important to get past your temporary concerns to reach your ultimate plan of raising a family. To put it bluntly, just hold your nose and jump! Good luck!

Preparing For Your New Arrival

Expecting a baby in the next few months? Here are some pointers for preparing yourself for the new arrival.

If you work outside of the home, plan to take off from work as early as you can. I know this isn't always possible. But moms who work up to the last minute of their pregnancies are often more restless and less able to relax when Junior arrives.

Establish your support system before Baby comes. Find friends (possibly those in a Lamaze or other childcare class) who are also pregnant or have just given birth. You'll be able to help each other through tough times, answer questions that may arise and simply enjoy the early months with a new baby.

If you're new to the area, contact your obstetrician or pediatrician to learn the names of local moms' groups. It's easy for isolated moms to feel lonely and frustrated with their infants. Don't be afraid to reach out and make those important contacts.

Rest as much as possible these last few months. Don't take on any new projects. Instead, store up sleep for later when you're apt to be up much of the night.

Get Junior's room ready early. You can never predict how you'll feel those last weeks. And more than one baby has surprised its parents by arriving ahead of schedule.

Going back to work soon after the birth? It's not too soon to arrange for childcare. Start interviewing now so you don't feel rushed at the end of your maternity leave.

Decide who you want to help you when you're home with Baby. It's certainly not a requirement, but it's awfully nice to have someone you trust to assist with meals, household chores and other children. Dad may want to take several days off, or Grandma may be able to lend a hand. But if you and your mom aren't on the best of terms, don't feel pressured into having her visit. A friend or hired helper will work as well.

Whatever you do, don't plan on entertaining visitors when you're first home from the hospital. Many well-meaning relatives have shown up two days after a baby's arrival, expecting to be entertained during their stay. Kindly let people know you'll call them when you're up to having house guests.

In fact, don't plan on doing much of anything for the first few months after Baby comes. The biggest mistake I see new moms make is trying to do too much too soon. Your job is to rest and get acquainted with your new family member. Avoid volunteering to host Uncle Bob's 45th birthday, or that surprise shower for a girlfriend.

Don't misunderstand me. Many women feel great after their deliveries, and can't wait to get back on their feet. But others take longer to recover, have difficulties with their infants or simply don't want any more responsibilities. There's no way you can predict how your labor, delivery and baby will be. It's better to not make any plans, than to realize you've taken on too much.

Buy yourself a new outfit or two to wear after you've delivered. Pick clothes a size or two larger than normal, with elasticized waists or wrap-around skirts. Nobody wants to wear maternity clothes again, but it's easy to feel discouraged because nothing else fits.

Don't get depressed about your body. Everybody feels like a beached whale during the last few months of pregnancy. But don't panic. With proper eating and exercise, your body *will* recover. Instead, focus on the amazing changes taking place, then relax and enjoy your new baby.

Preparing Siblings For New Baby's Arrival

Baby No. 2 has just arrived, and Mom and Dad couldn't be happier. But what can you do to help Baby No.1 adapt to the stork's little package?

Begin by including brothers and sisters as much as possible in the pregnancy. Read books together about the developing baby, listen to its heartbeat at the doctor's and include siblings in as many decisions as you can.

Asking questions such as, "Should we put the crib here or here?" lets older tots know they're important, too.

Avoid making negative statements to brothers and sisters about what a new baby will be like.

I heard one dad tell his child, "Well, Luke, the fun's almost over for you." He was not only forecasting doom and gloom for his son when his sibling arrived, but telling him his status was going to slip, too.

Instead, share positive feelings with your existing kids. "Caitlin, I was just as excited about your arrival as I am about our new baby's," allows her to share in your joy, while knowing she created equal happiness when she was born.

Don't worry if Junior doesn't share your enthusiasm for the upcoming arrival. He may express it openly: "I don't want a baby brother or sister." Or he may do it covertly, perhaps saying he'll throw Baby in the trash when it gets there.

Avoid saying, "You really don't hate this baby." Instead, say, "Daddy and I understand it's hard when a new person enters the family. But that doesn't mean we don't love you. In fact, we think you're TERRIFIC!"

It's imperative to protect your newborn from possible aggression from older siblings. It's not uncommon for toddlers to want to hurt an infant. But a jealous tot needs your help in controlling her anger.

Don't over react and lose your temper. That will only make your child, who is already feeling out of control since the baby's arrival, feel even more chaotic. Instead, set very firm limits about how Baby is to be handled.

Siblings may gently touch the new baby, but hitting, pulling or scratching are never allowed. Use time-outs and separations when aggressions occurs, and reward often when a sibling is gentle.

If anger continues, allow brothers and sisters safe outlets for those feelings. For example, they may want to hit a stuffed toy or doll. Or you can encourage them to draw pictures about their emotions.

Share your own feelings with your older children. Admit that you don't like it when Baby cries, either. Or tell them about a time you couldn't stand your own brother or sister when you were growing up. You'll not only be validating their emotions, you'll be soliciting them as partners in raising your new infant.

Make time when Baby naps for stories or projects with older siblings. And find special jobs requiring their skills. Thank them with sincere praise, letting them know you couldn't manage without them.

Don't forget that you, Mom, need to rest as much as possible, especially with two (or more) little ones around. The more you sleep and take care of yourself, the more patience you'll have to manage your days.

Finally, recognize adjusting to change is a regular occurrence in every youngster's life. Your children will adapt to their growing family. And the skills they acquire in this process will assist them throughout their years.

Macho Motherhood
Mothers in Contention for Top Honors

"Macho motherhood" is a parenting phenomenon characterized by an urgency to be the best possible parent, and a subtle competition with other mothers over who is doing the best job of raising their children.

Mothers caught up in this syndrome are obsessed with raising their children the "right" way. They are inordinately concerned with saying correct phrases to their youngsters, or using perfect discipline techniques.

"Macho mothers" constantly compare themselves and their children to other moms and their tots. "Am I feeding my toddler as healthy a lunch as they are?" they may question. Or "Is her daughter in a better pre-school than mine?"

"Macho mothers" feel compelled to have outstanding pregnancies, post-partum periods and breastfeeding experiences. They often push themselves to exercise until they deliver their babies, then return to the gym in a few weeks to regain their pre-pregnancy shapes.

"Macho mothers" also feel an unspoken pride about their child-bearing successes and tots' accomplishments. "Oh, yes, I breastfed Naomi until she was three," casually announced one mother. "I swam two miles the day before Jody was born," boasted another.

"Macho motherhood" is a fairly recent phenomenon. Professional women who have put jobs on hold to stay home with their children often suffer from a loss of identity. "Who am I if I'm not an office manager (or accountant, or systems analyst)?" they may wonder. They may turn their "get-ahead" philosophy into their mothering, as if proving to themselves they're still worthwhile.

Mothers continuing in the work place may feel guilty about spending long hours away from their tots. They may attempt to make up for lost time by being overly good parents.

Even non-professional women may become competitive in their parenting, subtly comparing themselves with other mothers to see how they stack up.

Dads appear immune to "macho motherhood". They have traditionally defined themselves in areas other than child-rearing, such as athletics, income or job status. As a result, they are less anxious and competitive about their parenting than their spouses.

The results of "macho motherhood" are many. Moms feel stressed, anxious and exhausted. And their incessant drives for perfection make them less tolerant and nurturing with their youngsters.

Children of "macho mothers" are often over-stimulated and burdened with excessive expectations. They may even grow resentful of the demands foisted upon them.

Now, I'm not advocating that mothers do anything less than what they feel is best for their children. And, certainly, each mother should follow her own physical and psychological guidelines in terms of energy, drive and stamina.

The problem develops when mothers feel compelled to maintain an unrealistic standard for themselves and their families. The wonderful--and chaotic--experience of raising children is turned into a contest in which no one wins.

How can you tell if you are a victim of "macho motherhood"? Ask yourself the following questions:

*Do I feel guilty about how I'm raising my children?

*Do I often compare myself to other mothers?

*Is it important I prove my worth as a mother to others?

*Am I very concerned about raising my children the "right" way?

If you answered 'yes' to any of these questions, you may be headed for "macho motherhood".

But don't despair. Simply remind yourself that children don't need perfect, gold medal mothers. They don't care about intelligence, weight or education. All they want is someone who is nurturing, calm and dependable, who makes them feel safe and utterly adored.

Acknowledging Life's Stages

Has your baby been an infant forever? Do you long for the good old days before children when you could wear clothes marked "dry clean only"?

In a recent discussion I lead at a new mom's group, the participants spoke openly about their struggles and frustrations during their children's early years.

For example, Sharon confessed dreading the clutter and chaos inherent in raising her two daughters, ages two and three months. "I can't get anything done during the day," she explained. "I'm further behind in the evening than I am when I wake up. It would be easier if I went back to work."

Another member, Lynnette, was on leave from her job at an advertising agency to stay home with her baby, Will. "I went to school to get a good job. But now I feel that my career is passing me by while I sit watching Barney."

These women loved their babies, and were pleased with their decisions to become parents. But they were still feeling a sense of stagnation. Their tots' early years were seemingly endless. They wondered if they would ever talk "grown up" again.

What may help ease these new mothers' dilemma is the awareness that women's lives are lived in segments. Unlike men, who may stay with a given career from graduation through retirement, women tend to fulfill various aspects of their lives in increments of five, ten or even fifteen years.

For instance, a woman may spend ten to fifteen years receiving an education, then five or ten years developing a career. During the mid-section of her life she may devote much of her energies to raising a family. And, when family commitments are less pressing, she may choose to pursue other activities.

Of course, this pattern is as unique as each woman herself. Many moms don't pursue outside employment, while others never take a break from their jobs.

The point is women's lives usually develop in blocks, rather than along linear pathways. There are specific chunks of time in their lives to experience specific events.

Rather than resenting an infant's constant nursing, recognize that, in only a few more years, the youngster will be off to school.

Instead of longing for a career temporarily put on hold, realize there will be plenty of time to head back to the office when parental duties are less pressing.

I'm certainly not meaning to diminish the tedium and stress many mothers experience when their children are tiny. Rather, I'm encouraging parents to see this time as a phase of life, teeming with temporary joys as well as temporary difficulties.

If you're still struggling with the pressures of new parenthood, try these helpful hints:

*Join a support group of other new mothers, or find supportive friends who are at the same stages of their lives. You'll be able to share parenting information and coping strategies.

*Take a class or read a book about the developmental stage of your child. You may discover those behaviors that are driving you crazy are actually very normal.

*Keep in mind babies and young children need love and patience more than a dust-free living room. Let some of your chores go so you can sit back and relax with the kids.

*Don't be too hard on yourself. Remember, you're new at this job. You're going to make mistakes.

*Finally, take regular breaks from your baby or toddler. I know it can be difficult, but you need time to recharge your battery. Having a paid sitter, a neighbor or other mom take over for an hour can make all the difference in your sanity.

Sharing
A Challenge for Every Tot

"Mine! Mine!" screams two year-old Augusta for the fiftieth time that morning.

As her tiny face reddens with frustration, and her eyes well with tears, it's hard to see who's having the harder time, Augusta or her mother.

Sharing is a struggle for all toddlers and their families. Whatever they see, they want. Whatever they have, they want to keep.

They feel threatened by other tots reaching for toys in their clutches, but have no trouble grabbing other toddlers' treasures.

This phenomenon is especially acute when other kids are over to play.

For instance, when two year-old Jamie had a friend, Kyle, over to play, he spent the afternoon desperately protecting his toys from his perceived intruder. If Kyle reached for the dump truck, Jamie dashed over to snatch it. As Kyle headed for the push toy, Jamie dropped the truck to seize that, too.

The more Mom pleaded with Jamie to, "Share nicely," the more frantic he became. Jamie's mother was embarrassed by her son's behavior, and Jamie felt frustrated and out of control.

What can you do to minimize sharing trauma for both parents and toddlers during this stage?

Start by acknowledging the fact that every youngster has difficulty sharing. It's no reflection on your parenting ability, and it's not a character flaw in your child.

View learning to share as an ongoing process of gaining self-control. They won't master the skill overnight. But, with maturity and patient guidance, they do get better at it.

Avoid losing your temper over their outbursts. Since you're teaching them how to stay in control, it's important to model the same behavior. When Serena started hitting her friend to get her toy back, her mother calmly told Serena she could not hit another child. Mother encouraged Serena to use her words to find a solution to their problem. This approach not only soothed over Serena's anger, but taught her an important lesson in getting along with others.

Talk with children about sharing strategies before friends arrive. Discuss which toys are too special to share with visitors, and put those out of sight until after the other children have left. Explain that the remaining toys will all be shared. Let your tot know you'll be there to smooth over disagreements.

Use a kitchen timer to help diminish sharing squabbles. For instance, if both tots want the paint set, let Kammy go first, and set the timer for 10 minutes. When the buzzer sounds, Stephanie gets a turn.

Often, by the time 10 minutes have elapsed, neither child wants the activity anymore. That's fine. You've momentarily defused their frustrations, and demonstrated a good way to share.

Praise your toddler when she's shared her toys. A sincere, "Good job, Monica. You've let Julie play with your ponies," lets her know she's been successful.

If you've tried these techniques, and your child still has trouble sharing, don't despair. These skills take time to develop. And this stage won't last forever.

Shopping With Your Youngsters

Tips for Making it Through the Store

Rosemary and her four year-old granddaughter, Stacy, are in the grocery store. At the dairy section, Stacy starts playing with a nearby display of stuffed animals. "Don't touch those, Dear," Rosemary calls sweetly, as she picks up a container of low-fat milk.

Stacy ignores her grandmother, and begins pulling teddy bears off their racks. "Stacy, listen to Grandma. Put those back," admonishes Rosemary, still searching the shelves for items on her shopping list.

Finally, Stacy topples the display to the floor, spilling toys across the aisle. "You naughty girl! I'm so ashamed!" scolds Rosemary, now feeling exasperated and embarrassed. "You're going to get a spanking when we get home!"

Shopping with youngsters can be a challenge. But there are steps you can take to minimize the hassles and maximize the chances that your trip to the store will be a success.

Start by making sure both you and your kids are in a good mood. Don't attempt the store if any of you are tired, rushed, ill or generally out of sorts. It's far better to do without the items than to risk possible disaster.

Tell your children how you want them to behave before you get into the store. Explain one or two simple rules you expect to be followed. For example, you may require that they not take anything off the shelves, that they touch the cart at all times or that you will not buy them a treat.

If appropriate, practice the rules with the kids on the way into the store so they fully understand what you want them to do. For instance, Rosemary might have instructed Stacy to stay by her side in the store, then the two of them could have walked together from the car.

Correct youngsters' misbehaviors immediately. Don't wait until they're out of control before trying to reign them in. Rather, remind them promptly, using a gentle but firm voice, that they're not meeting the specified expectations.

Don't attempt to correct children from a distance, or before you have their full attention. Kids focus on what is nearest and most interesting to them. Therefore, it's best to stop what you are doing, go over to your youngsters and make sure they're tuned in to what you're saying.

When Rosemary found Stacy completely absorbed by the stuffed toys, she should have stopped what she was doing, walked over to Stacy, and either bent down to talk to her, or laid her hand on her granddaughter's shoulder. "Stacy, you may not touch the toys. Please take Grandma's hand and come back to the shopping cart."

Enlist your youngsters' help in the store. For example, you can ask your toddler for suggestions for planning dinner. Your pre-schooler can count out the desired number of bananas. An older child can get items for you in another aisle.

When possible, make shopping a game. For instance, you might tell your kids, "I'm in a real hurry today. Let's set our watches and see how quickly we can gather up all this stuff."

Praise your youngsters when they're cooperative. In fact, it doesn't hurt to praise squirmy, soon-to-be-restless toddlers after every aisle to keep them from getting bored. Phrases such as, "Ryan, you are being such a help to Grandpa!" not only let kids know you approve of how they're behaving, but create a positive atmosphere that minimizes fatigue and grouchiness.

Use caution when buying children candy, toys or other treats while you're in the store. Sure, an occasional goody may be warranted. However, it's easy to fall into the "Mommy-can-you-buy-me-something?" trap. To avoid that problem, clearly explain your treats policy before beginning to shop. Then stick with it. Don't let a whiny toddler coerce you into buying a sucker. And never let kids sneak unapproved goodies into the cart. Your children may grumble and call you "Attila." But your consistency will reward you in the end.

Chapter 11

Teens And Adolescents

"Youth is wholly experimental."

Robert Louis Stevenson
1850-1894

Making Good Decisions

Making good decisions is as important a skill as using a computer or driving a car. But, as with any skill, it requires patience and practice to perfect it.

Below are eight rules for making good decisions. They won't necessarily make the choices you face any easier. But they will help you tackle them with more courage and self-confidence.

Gather information. Find out as much as you can about all the choices you're facing. For example, if you're deciding where to go to college, read lots of college catalogues, talk with other professionals to find out where they went to school and discuss with your counselor which schools have the programs you're most interested in. When it comes to making good decisions, information is power.

Decide what's important to you. After gathering all the information, analyze which facts are relevant to you. If you're deciding about what after-school activity you want to participate in, ask yourself what you want from an activity. Are you most interested in doing something physical? Can you work it around your schedule? Do your friends also participate? Write these criteria down in order of importance, then see which activities best meet your needs.

Make one decision at a time. It's easy to get over loaded and confused when making important decisions, so only make one at a time. For example, if you're deciding which kind of dog you want for a family pet, don't also try to design the dog house, buy the kennel and select the vet at the same time.

<u>Keep it simple</u>. Avoid complicating the decision with lots of mental clutter, such as needless worry or concern about the future. Those only cause anxiety and confusion about the real issue at hand. Since none of us can predict what will happen tomorrow, base the decision on the best information you have today.

<u>Listen to your feelings</u>. Much of the time, we already know what we should do. But we complicate the problem with so many extraneous issues that the answer gets lost in the chaos.

If we allow ourselves to be still, take a few deep breaths and listen to our true feelings, a seemingly difficult matter may become clear. The answer may not be what we want, but it may be what is best.

<u>Recognize no decision is perfect</u>. Think of decisions in terms of percentages. Ask yourself, "What percentage favors this choice? What percentage favors another?" Then, pick the choice with the highest percentage.

Some decisions are fairly obvious, perhaps 70 % to 30 %. But others are more difficult, say 55 % to 45 %. Allow yourself to select the one with the highest rating. Part of you will be disappointed. But you want to make the decision that will minimize your disappointment and maximize your benefit.

<u>Set a time limit for making a decision</u>. Some decisions have automatic deadlines, such as college applications. But others, such as deciding to move out on your own, can drag on forever. Give yourself a reasonable time to ponder, then go ahead and choose.

Let's say you and your boyfriend have been having problems and you're trying to decide whether or not you should break up with him. Set a date, perhaps two months from now, to see if the relationship has improved. If, by then, things haven't gotten any better, you'll know it's time to end it.

<u>Don't look back</u>. Make a decision, then move on. Don't second guess yourself. Even if you make what turns out to be the wrong choice, realize you made the best one you could based on the information available to you at the time. Don't beat yourself up about something that's already past, and over which you have no control. Save your emotional energy for tackling the next problem.

Teen-age Sexual Abstinence
Guiding Your Teen to Make Positive Choices

Teen-age sexual abstinence has gotten a bad rap. The term has become laden with negative, drastic and rigid connotations. Just saying the word is apt to make a teen feel deprived.

But rather than viewing abstinence as a prison sentence, it should be seen as a choice of lifestyle. Just as eating a healthy diet or not smoking cigarettes or drinking alcohol are positive decisions that require choosing certain options over others, the choice of sexual abstinence can be a series of options involving every facet of a young person's life.

Sexual abstinence does not deny that a teen has sexual feelings. In fact, one of the most important aspects of the teen years is to understand and be comfortable with one's sexuality. But within that comfort comes a knowledge of the right times and ways to express sexual love, and the wisdom to choose suitable partners.

What can parents and their teens do to support the decision of abstinence? Begin by making a contract that abstinence will be the lifestyle of choice. Parents, you can't make this one for your kids. But you can compassionately offer input and guidance.

Discuss the rationale behind sexual abstinence. Sure, fear of disease and unwanted pregnancy are important. But the real issue lies even deeper.

Sexual expression is the most intimate relationship a couple can share. Relegating it to nervous and hasty encounters in cars or unattended rooms not only degrades the partners involved, but eliminates all sense of love and caring--the true reason for sexual expression.

Once that decision has been arrived at, lay out a plan together to make it work. Abstinence is far more than saying "No," in a moment of heated passion. It takes planning and effort. Don't leave it to chance.

Explore your child's personal goals. Kids with clear-cut aspirations are less likely to get side-tracked by next week's party or Saturday's good-looking date.

Don't ask, "What are you doing about your future?" Most teens don't know what they're doing the next week, much less throughout their whole lives. Instead, help teens decide what they want to accomplish this next semester or year. What do they have to do to get there? What can parents do to support their efforts?

Friends are a crucial factor in the success or failure of your teen's plan. Those with similar convictions will be supportive; those without will work against her. Of course, your teen must pick her own friends. But if she understands the role they play in the success of her goals, she may choose them a little more wisely.

Group activities are great ways to be with friends and still support the decision of abstinence. Church groups, school activities and athletic events are fun, and minimize the chances of being put in compromising situations.

Discuss ahead of time what teens can do if they feel uncomfortable in a situation. Role-play phrases and actions they can say or use. Encourage them to phone home if necessary.

Parents, don't forget your role in the support of sexual abstinence. Just because teens appear mature does not mean they don't need adult supervision. Follow your instincts. Don't let your teens go to parties when adults aren't present. Don't let teens spend time alone in your home. Be available to talk to your child.

The topic of sexual abstinence is difficult and controversial. I don't expect all of you to agree with my suggestions. My wish is that these ideas spur you and your teen-agers to discuss possible lifestyle changes that will lead to wise decisions.

Teen Dating
Learning To Pick Good Partners

Teens, this column's for you. You're entering your dating years and beginning to develop relationships with the opposite gender. Now is a good time to ask yourself the question: "What characteristics should I look for in a partner?"

Of course, most teen-agers aren't in the market for a spouse. You've got better things to think about than settling down with just one person. But wisely choosing a boyfriend or a girlfriend is a skill. And just as you're developing other skills in literature, algebra and basketball, now's the time to practice your interpersonal skills, too. You may not realize it, but the patterns you establish for relationships at this stage of your life will stay with you and help you when the selections you make will be more permanent.

What should you consider when picking a partner? The most obvious element is attraction, both physical *and* emotional. Sure, you want to like how that person looks. But it's equally important to like how he or she acts. People change all throughout their lives. They mature, age and sometimes even have accidents or illnesses that alter their appearances. Relationships based solely on great looks usually struggle when beauty begins to fade.

Choose a person who respects you. This includes respecting your body, your beliefs, your interests, your opinions... everything. Never stay with a partner who in any way physically or verbally abuses you. No matter what you may have done, or no matter what a person tells you, you never deserve to be hit, slapped, verbally belittled or coerced into doing something you are uncomfortable with. Never. A person who does so is bad news and is unlikely to change without lots of counseling. Move on to someone else.

Look for a partner who shares common interests and activities with you. You may like the same sport, belong to the same temple, enjoy studying foreign languages or share a love of nature. The more interests you share, the more you'll have in common. And couples who have lots in common find it easier to weather the down times that challenge all relationships.

Do you like this person's friends and do they like you? If you're having to abandon all your former friends, or sneak meetings with this girl- or boyfriend so your buddies don't get mad, then something's not right. Use this as a cue to find someone who likes the same people as you do.

Do you and this boy or girl share mutual goals? Do you both aspire to roughly the same levels of education or similar levels of professional achievement? Do you see your lives progressing in approximately the same directions? Of course, no two people are going to be clones. But the closer your future plans are, the less disagreements you are likely to have.

Choose someone with a similar degree of religious conviction. You may want to select a partner from within your faith, or you may be comfortable crossing denominational lines. Whichever you decide, a partner of equal devoutness (or lack of devoutness) is more apt to be compatible with you than someone of very diverse beliefs.

I know there are many successful relationships that haven't followed all the rules. But my experience as a marriage and family counselor has shown me these are some of the factors that promote healthy unions. Also, keep in mind these criteria are only guidelines. They are not cast in concrete. Some of them will be more appropriate to you than others, so use them as tools for considering potential dates.

Chapter 12

•

Grandparents And Grandchildren

"The younger generation will be knocking at my door."

Henrik Ibsen
1828-1906

Custodial Grandparents
When Grandparents Become Mom and Dad

Custodial Grandparents are grandparents who are raising their grandchildren on a full-time, custodial basis. Whether as a result of their own children's divorce, death, drug abuse or other physical or emotional incapacities, more and more grandparents are finding themselves in the roles of Mom and Dad.

Custodial Grandparents face unique challenges. The most obvious one is age. The demands of active toddlers or boisterous adolescents can be trying to the healthiest, most vigorous of parents. When they're foisted upon grandparents in their forties, fifties, sixties or even seventies, the result can cause the grandparents excessive fatigue, anxiety, impatience and feelings of being overwhelmed.

Custodial Grandparents are often dealing with their own intense grief over the death or loss of functioning of their child. They may experience profound guilt about that person's failure to raise his or her own family, wondering, "How could we have prevented this tragedy?"

Custodial Grandparents may harbor intense anger or frustration over their situation. They may have planned and saved their whole lives for retirement, a retirement they must now put on hold because the grandchildren are in their lives.

To make matters even more complex, the grandchildren these Custodial Grandparents must raise are often the products of drug- and alcohol-abusing parents, and may possess serious emotional, physical or educational problems. For example, Ruth and Harold's two young grandsons, who both have learning disabilities, attended eight different schools before their mother sought treatment for her drug addiction, and relinquished custody of the children to her parents.

Finally, Custodial Grandparents have minimal support in their roles of raising grandchildren. For instance, they may have nothing in common with the other parents of their grandchildren's friends. When Marsha, in her early fifties, took five year-old Lonnie to her swim class, she felt uncomfortable chatting with the much younger parents of the other students.

They may even disassociate themselves from friends their own ages who aren't interested in attending dance recitals or being around pre-schoolers.

How can you cope with the challenge of being a Custodial Grandparent? Start by acknowledging that your situation will never be perfect. You can only do the best you can.

Recognize yourself as a blessing to your grandchildren. Sure, you'll have ups and downs with the kids. You may even be pulling out your hair. Don't worry. The grandkids are lucky you stepped in to raise them. They may just not feel that way now.

Create structure in their environment. Have regular mealtimes, storytimes, bedtimes and chores. Children with traumatic, chaotic backgrounds thrive on consistent guidelines and policies. Don't be afraid to put your foot down.

Take frequent breaks. Walk, nap in the afternoons, take up oil painting, go out to dinner without the grandchildren. Utilize baby-sitters frequently. You're no good to anyone if you're bitter and exhausted, so remember to recharge your personal batteries often.

Finally, don't forget the positive parts of your life. If being a Custodial Grandparent is particularly draining for you, allow yourself to participate in pleasurable hobbies or spend time with friends. You'll be showing your grandchildren skills in managing crises, as well as conveying the message, "We're all in this together. Somehow we'll survive."

Find support from other Custodial Grandparents. You may choose to be involved in a local organization at your grandchild's school or at church. Or you may wish to contact Grandparents Who Care, in San Francisco, phone number (415) 664-4757, or The Grandparent Information Center in Washington, D.C., phone number (202) 434-2296.

Managing Visiting Grandchildren

The grandkids are coming for the holidays. And, while almost all visiting relatives are stressful, visiting children can be disastrous.

For example, your standards and expectations may differ from those of the youngsters' parents. Actions allowed in their homes may not be acceptable in yours.

Your house may not be kid-proof. Fragile breakables on the coffee table can be tempting to young tots. Light colors and delicate fabrics can be impractical for active bodies.

How can you insure you and your house survive intact? Start by securing the premises. Put away all those delicate knick-knacks, especially if toddlers are coming.

Provide an area where children can play. It may be a corner of a guest bedroom, or a kitchen counter. Supply age-appropriate toys or quiet activities in a nearby closet or drawer. Let youngsters know they are welcome to play in these areas, but they need to take care of the supplies. Keep in mind that the more captivating the toys, the longer they'll hold young attentions.

Make outdoor activities available. A croquet set on the lawn, a basketball hoop on the driveway or a push toy for the sidewalk can keep small feet off the sofa, and help burn off excess energy.

Ask athletic relatives to organize frisbee contests or baseball games at a nearby park or school. You'll be protecting your cherished roses while providing opportunities for family fun.

Don't hesitate to establish your own rules for your home. For example, remind grandchildren they must walk while they're indoors, or wipe their feet before coming inside.

If they respond, "But it's OK at our house," gently explain, "At Grandma's, we have different rules."

Don't worry about being an ogre. You'll be teaching the kids some manners while maintaining your sanity and furnishings.

Elicit the children's parents as allies, especially if they've been uncooperative in the past. Call them before the event, and ask how they think the youngsters can best be entertained during their visit. Let the folks know you want to see them, but that you understand how restless young ones can get. There's no guarantee the parents will jump to your assistance. But at least you'll have done your best.

If you've tried all these suggestions, and the kids are still too hard on your home, examine your standard of living. Perhaps your surroundings aren't right for multi-generational gatherings. Or maybe the strain of so many guests has become too great. If this is the case, consider relocating festivities to another, more durable environment.

Chapter 13

Violence And Gangs

"Violence and injury enclose in their net all that do such things, and generally return upon him who began."

Lucretius
99-55 B. C.

Steps For Minimizing Childhood Violence

We're all concerned about the increase of violent acts committed by children. But you can minimize the potential for violence in your youngsters by following these suggestions:

* Treat your children non-violently. Children treat others in the same way they are treated at home. If you want to raise non-violent sons and daughters, you must use respectful, non-violent methods for communication and discipline. When parents hit or yell at their youngsters, they are sending them clear messages that it's OK to use aggression against others.

* Recognize some violence is innate in children. Very young boys will fashion guns out of anything they can get their hands on. And boys of all ages enjoy wrestling with their buddies or whacking things with sticks. Our job as parents is not to eliminate violent tendencies entirely, but rather to channel these energies into productive, acceptable activities.

* Teach your children how to solve problems non-violently. Kids need to know aggression is *never* the right way to handle a disagreement, and they need to develop their problem-solving skills.

For example, you can help a pre-schooler share her toys with her friends by discussing sharing strategies before her friends come over. Or you can help grade-schoolers handle a playground dispute by leading them to explore alternative solutions to their squabble.

* Limit your children's exposure to television, videos and violent movies. Young viewers of aggressive shows become desensitized to the suffering of others. Bombings, murders, dismemberments and rapes become ho-hum events. If children do watch TV, encourage them to select shows that depict non-violent themes, and portray characters behaving peacefully toward others.

* Model gentle treatment of pets and other animals. Never intentionally frighten or harm an animal, especially in front of young children. Instead, show youngsters how to safely hold a pet in their hands, or quietly observe wild animals from a distance.

* Disallow the purchase of violent or offensive products, even with your child's own money. Instead, help your son or daughter find similar items that are acceptable.

* Direct children toward non-violent hobbies. Playing a musical instrument, participating in sports, collecting stamps and raising animals are all examples of constructive, non-violent activities.

* Model non-violent expressions of anger. Show your children how to use a punching bag, go for a jog, scream into a pillow or take a long walk to safely let off steam.

If this is a problem area for you or your spouse, take a class in anger management, or get help from a professional. You'll be doing everyone in your family a big service.

* Don't glorify violent activities, such as aggressive sporting events, big game hunting or war-related activities. I'm not saying these pastimes are inherently

bad. But when they become a family's primary focus, they may encourage other, more violent acts.

* Teach your children to accept responsibility for their actions. Perpetrators of violent acts often blame their victims, claiming, "He made me do it." Instead, kids need to know *nobody* makes them do anything. They always have choices about how they will respond in any situation. They are ultimately responsible for every outcome.

Discouraging Children From Joining Gangs

Joe Quiroz is the Gang Specialist at the El Paso de Robles School, a state operated school for juvenile offenders, in Paso Robles, California. He and Assistant Principal Russ Harris developed the following tips for keeping kids away from gangs. Their ideas first appeared in the Newsletter of the Associated American Karate Systems, and are presented here with their permission.

<u>HOW TO DISCOURAGE YOUR CHILDREN FROM JOINING GANGS</u>

1) Discourage your children from hanging around with gang members. Kids are easily influenced by their peers. If your children choose friends who are mostly from gangs, chances are high they will become involved, too. Make an effort to meet and get to know your children's friends. Learn how they spend their free time, and what influences they exert over your youngsters.

2) Occupy your children's free time. Bored kids are often headed for trouble. Get your youngsters involved in after-school activities, sports, city recreation or church programs. Make sure they have plenty of age-appropriate responsibilities at home, too.

3) Develop good communication with your children. Good communication is open, frequent and positive. It

allows your youngsters to approach you with any topic or problem. Good communication does not condemn kids. Instead, it offers an avenue to convey to them how much you love them.

4) Spend time with your children. Kids need their parents' time. They need to do things as a family and to share time one-on-one. Take them on trips to different places outside of your neighborhood. Visit parks, museums, the beach, the mountains--anywhere!

5) Do not buy or allow your children to dress in gang style clothing. Youngsters who dress in gang style clothing are expressing an interest in gangs and will attract the attention of gang members.

6) Set limits with your children. Kids need to know what is acceptable and unacceptable behavior. It's never too early to start teaching them.

7) Do not allow your children to stay out late at night, or to spend lots of unsupervised time at home or out on the streets.

8) Do not allow your children to write or practice writing gang names, symbols or any other gang graffiti on walls or on their books, papers, clothes or bodies.

9) Develop an anti-gang environment in your home. Clearly and continually express your disapproval of gang activity, and of any family members joining gangs.

10) Learn about gang and drug activity in your community. Learn how gang members dress, speak and act. Attend informational meetings, and read articles related to gang activities. Become an informed parent!

11) Participate in your children's education. Take an interest in your youngsters' school activities. Help them with their homework. Visit their schools, meet their teachers and attend parent-school meetings. Set high academic standards.

12) Get involved in your community. Know your neighbors. Organize or join neighborhood watch groups. Discourage gangs from hanging around your neighborhood. Remove graffiti near your home. Attend community functions. Teach your children civic pride.

13) Be a good example by becoming an active parent.

Chapter 14

Sports And Family Fitness

"Young and old come forth to play
On a sunshine holiday."

John Milton
1608-1674

Fit Kids, Healthy Kids

Fit kids are healthy kids, both physically and mentally.

A recent study at the University of Idaho reported active youngsters have more friends and are more outgoing than their inactive classmates. It went on to show that, especially after third grade, the least lonely children were above average in their levels of activity and fitness, while the loneliest were more sedate and out of shape.

Unfortunately, kids are becoming less physically active. A survey conducted by the U.S. Public Health Service examined the way children, ages six to nine, spent their time in school, at home and in the community. The study found youngsters are not getting the right kinds of exercise, are significantly fatter than kids a generation ago and spend more time watching television than in physical activity.

The research showed that, while nearly all early elementary school children took physical education at school, only one-third of those youngsters did so on a daily basis. And most of the programs emphasized sports, rather than health and exercise habits.

But parents, take heart! You can help reverse these trends. Government studies point out that kids who exercise with Mom and Dad are in better shape than their peers. The message is clear: If we take the time to exercise with our sons and daughters, we'll be directing them toward fitness and health.

How can you exercise with your children?

Start by finding activities you can all do together. Great family recreation can include swimming, hiking, riding bikes, camping, horseback riding or assorted ball games. The possibilities are endless.

Gear the activities to the ages of your children. Toddlers and pre-schoolers love the park and the beach. Elementary school-age youngsters are ready for more organized games, such as baseball, beginning sports such as tennis, hiking, camping and riding bikes. Teens love volleyball, backpacking, camping, jogging and aerobics.

Have fun. The goal is to foster life-long habits of good health and fitness, not examine every flaw in someone's game. Keep the atmosphere light, and make sure everyone is having a good time.

If your child is pursuing sports on a more serious level, for example gymnastics or soccer, practice together, but save most coaching for the coach. Parent-child coaching relationships are tricky. It's best for most parents to stay on the sidelines.

It's never too early too start. While I'm not a big believer in organized sports for children under seven, tiny tots can roll big balls, push carts and play on structures. Giving them plenty of physical, outdoor play starts them on the path to fitness.

Plan active family vacations. For instance, you can rent a cabin in the mountains, and learn canoeing as a family.

If working-out with Junior doesn't provide enough exercise for you, then work-out after you've played with him. Or have him ride his bike while you jog alongside. You can even design a kid-sized weight-lifting routine so the two of you can pump iron together.

Remember, not all exercise has to be grueling. A fun game of catch, a gentle stroll through the park, a walk on the beach while tossing sticks to the family dog or a wild game of tag on the lawn are all fitness promoting activities.

Turn off the TV. Not only is watching television a sedentary activity, but many kids snack while they watch. Do your whole family a big favor. Pull the plug, and go outside and play!

Don't Rush Children Into Sports

I am often asked the best age to start children in organized athletics. With the current emphasis being "the younger the better," many parents feel the need to sign their kids up for lessons as early as four, five or six years old.

My thinking is somewhat different. I contend that the best time to begin sports is around eight or nine.

Most eight or nine year-olds possess the physical strength and coordination to control their own bodies. For example, their reflexes are developed enough to allow them to catch a basketball without getting hit in the face. Their hands are strong enough to let them grip a tennis racquet. Younger children aren't as physically mature, and are more likely to feel frustrated with their inabilities.

Youngsters in this older age group have long enough attention spans so they can follow directions from a teacher or a coach. They can carry out a series of instructions or run through drills without becoming confused. They can usually practice a skill several times in a row, or for a determined length of time, allowing them to progress at a faster rate than younger tots.

I know tennis coaches who offer classes for youngsters barely out of diapers, promising parents future pros by the time the kids are teens. And, while the pre-schoolers may indeed have fun, when they reach third grade, they will be at about the same level as their fellow students just taking up the sport.

Of course, there are exceptions. A child with exceptional ability or interest may be given formal instruction at an earlier age. But even then, caution is required. Too many childhood phenoms are either burned out or injured by the time they should be reaching the pinnacles of their sports. I'd rather have a child start a little later, and enjoy the activity a lot longer.

This is not to say kids should be couch potatoes until halfway through grammar school. Of course not! But rather than receiving formal lessons, they should be developing their gross motor coordination. Throwing large soft balls, swimming, riding tricycles and bikes, climbing jungle gyms and going for walks are all excellent ways to build the strength and stamina needed for sports later on.

When kids do start in sports, I advise parents to de-emphasize overall performance and focus instead on skills that are appropriate for the child's ability. One wise youth baseball coach I know isn't concerned that his third- and fourth-graders successfully complete their catches. Instead, he encourages them to simply touch each ball with their mitts. His young athletes are improving their speed and depth perception without the pressure of dropping the ball.

Always support players' efforts over their performances. Very few ever make the big play or sink the game-saving jump shot. But many can feel the exhilaration of participation and physical success. Even when children are destined to be perennial bench warmers, supporting their commitment and dedication can make them feel like heroes.

Let children dictate their levels of involvement in their activities. You may expose them to a sport, but allow them to determine how much effort they want to put into it. I've watched too many parents pour countless hours and dollars into their children's sports only to feel anger and resentment when the youngsters give less than their best.

The goal of youth sports is to develop lifelong habits of good health and recreation. Starting kids at the right age--and with the proper attitude--establishes the groundwork for a successful and satisfying athletic experience.

Coaching Your Youngster In Sports

Many parents want to coach their sons and daughters in sports. But coaching your own kids can be tricky. Ask yourself the following questions, then tally up your score. You'll find out fast if you have first-string possibilities, or are better suited for the bench.

<u>Do you have a good knowledge of the sport?</u> You needn't have been an Olympian, but coaching does require a rudimentary understanding of fundamentals, rules and strategies. This groundwork becomes even more important as youngsters advance in age and abilities.

If you played your sport competitively in high school or college, or have some special training or experience in coaching this activity, score yourself 5 points. If you have a pretty good idea how the game is played, and are motivated to learn more about it, give yourself 3 points. If you haven't a clue about what you're doing, you get 1 point in this category.

<u>Do you place your child's physical and emotional development ahead of his or her athletic success?</u> Sure, we all like to win. But the goals of childhood athletics should be to help kids strengthen their bodies and learn sportsmanship and etiquette, not embark on a win-at-all-costs crusade. Boys and girls should be encouraged to be gracious in both victory and defeat. Competition may be a part of athletics, but it should not be the primary purpose.

Analyze your own personality. If you are most interested in seeing your youngster have a positive experience, regardless of the score, then give yourself 5 points. If you really like to win, but think you can keep the game in perspective, give yourself 3 points. If you head right for the throat in any sort of contest, you get 1 point.

Do you and your child work well together? Coaching your kids should be fun. It should not turn into a power struggle. Of course, there will be moments when they goof off a little, or need to have you focus their attention. But your relationship should feel closer as a result of the experience, not damaged.

If you and your youngster usually have a good time together, you get 5 points here. If he or she goofs off sometimes because you're the coach, but mostly enjoys having you around, give yourself 3 points. If your child turns sulky, cries or threatens to quit during your sessions, give yourself 1 point.

Does your child like having you as a coach? Look around. Is your daughter happy you're helping her learn a new dive? Is your son eager for you to help him with his pitching? If so, give yourself 5 points. If they don't mind, but occasionally want you to back off, give yourself 3 points. If they're constantly begging to stop, give yourself 1 point.

How'd you do? If you scored over 15 points, then go get your game book and whistle, and head out to the courts. You'll probably have a great time coaching your child.

If you scored 10-14, then you probably have high interest and good intentions, but are lacking in one of the crucial areas. You may not be successful as the sole coach of your child, but you may prove useful in other areas. For example, you may want to shoot jump shots with your youngster on the driveway, or hit golf balls together at the practice range.

If your score was under 10 points, it's best to let someone else coach your child. The relationship just isn't right for the two of you. But that certainly doesn't exclude you from sports involvement. All kids need support from the sidelines in terms of carpools, uniforms, equipment and cheers. And never forget the best words you can share with your minor leaguer: "I love you. Have a good game."

Fitting Fitness Into Your Family

Want to make family fitness a priority in your household? Want to have fun being physically active as a family? Follow these suggestions to help you get on track:

Make enjoyment your number one goal. The priority of family fitness is for everyone to have fun, and to feel good about each other as a result of having participated.

Too often parents and spouses entice family members into an activity, then treat them like they're in boot camp.

Bert made this mistake with his wife, Jeri. Bert wanted Jeri to take up jogging with him. But every time she ran with him, he complained she was too slow. Rather than supporting Jeri's efforts to take up a new sport, he berated her for not keeping pace. Finally, Jeri refused to run with her husband.

Barb took a different approach with her 15 year-old son, Caleb.

Barb was teaching Caleb to play golf. But rather than criticizing his lack of skill, she praised his efforts on the course. She offered minimal suggestions, and instead made their outings pleasant and relaxed. Caleb was not destined to make the pro circuit, but he loved playing golf with his mom.

Select cooperative over competitive activities. Competitive activities tend to pit family members against one another. Only one person or team can win, so there are always people who lose and feel bad.

Cooperative activities, such as hiking, biking and camping, foster positive feelings among families. Everyone can be successful in the activity and feel satisfied with the results.

The Dailys, for example, were avid tennis players. When they played together as a family, winning was foremost in their minds. Unfortunately, scores took precedence over sportsmanship; tempers often grew heated, and cross words were sometimes exchanged. As a result, family members felt less affectionate toward each other after their matches. Their relationships were hindered, rather than helped, by their games.

The Johnsrud family, on the other hand, liked to backpack together. They helped each other pitch tents, cook meals and scout trails. When they climbed a peak, they would wait until they were all together before they made their final ascent. That way they *all* reached the top at the same time. Their relationships were regularly strengthened by their times in the mountains.

<u>Gear the activity to the youngest or least skilled member of the family</u>. Family activities must be geared to the levels of the participants to be successful. If you're skiing with a kindergartener, stay within that child's abilities. If you're cycling with novices, go only as far and fast as they can comfortably go.

I know this is difficult for you weekend Olympians, who don't do anything unless it's for a personal best. But remember, the goal of family fitness is fun, not world records. Leave your stop watch at home when you're out with your spouse and kids.

The best way to avoid frustrating both you and your family is to get your work-out in *before* you take them out. That way you won't be fretting about the time you're wasting at the park with your pre-schoolers or tossing tennis balls to your spouse who is just taking up the sport.

<u>Adapt traditional activities to accomodate your family's abilities</u>. Is your family not quite ready for a *real* game of baseball or golf? Then change an old-time favorite, or make up a brand new creation.

Our family recently participated in a multi-family version of soccer, played with a ball that was four feet in diameter. The men were not allowed to touch the ball with their hands, but the women and kids could pick it up and throw it (if they could!). We changed teams often, adapted rules as needed and didn't keep score. Our afternoon of "Redball" left us laughing, exhausted and great friends.

Chapter 15

•

Happy Holidays

"Who first invented work,
and bound the free
And holiday-rejoicing spirit down?"

Charles Lamb
1775-1834

Handling The Holidays
How Not To Be a Holiday Victim

We hear lots of talk about peace at Christmas. But few of us feel any of it in our lives this time of the year. We spend too much money, wait in too many lines and get too many headaches. But this time, try something different. Give yourself and your family a peaceful Christmas. It will be the best gift you ever gave.

A peaceful Christmas begins when you stop being a Holiday victim. Holiday victims dislike the hype and commercialism of the season, but feel helpless to do anything differently. They feel powerless to spend less money or to not attend family gatherings that always end in bickering. Instead, they suppress their own needs for sanity and calm, and follow what they perceive are external demands on their time and finances. Recognizing that you can make choices about how you celebrate the Holidays is the first step in regaining control

Decide what you and other family members want from your Holiday celebrations. Some families want Christmas to be a spiritual celebration. Others view it as a chance to buy great gifts. Still others take the time off from work to visit exotic places. There's no right or wrong way to do it. It's completely up to you.

Once you've decided what you want from Christmas, make plans that facilitate your needs. Buy tickets to that musical performance you've wanted to hear, or plan that get-together with friends.

Give yourself permission to not meet others' expectations if they conflict with your own needs. You may feel pressured to make a trip back to Missouri to visit family. But you may also realize how your own well-being hinges on being with your local family and friends. It's OK not to cave in to demands.

I'm certainly not advocating you ignore everyone but yourself. Instead, I'm encouraging you to recognize your own personal Holiday desires, and reach a compromise that works with others' needs.

Establish Holiday traditions. Traditions are familiar patterns we follow every year. Because of their repetition, we know what to expect, and are provided with a degree of comfort and stability. You may want to recreate some of the traditions you encountered as a child. Or you may want to start brand new ones that separate you from the past. You may choose to attend an annual performance of the Nutcracker, or simply sing a few carols around the fire. Whatever you select, recognize the soothing character of traditions, and incorporate them into your peaceful plan.

Find time for special moments with your family. For some reason, normally mundane events gain new significance during the Holidays. And, in our efforts to create that picture perfect Christmas, we miss our chance to experience the most precious times of all. A little boy warming his bottom by the fire after a bath deserves a loving hug. And Grandpa reading his evening paper warrants a quiet chat. I can still remember the fun my mother and I had making fudge for Christmas presents one year. I've given lots of gifts in my life, but I don't remember any as clearly as I do that candy. Those peaceful moments are the real core of Christmas. Don't get so wrapped up that you pass them by.

Minimize your Holiday expectations. I know this is difficult with all the media and commercial hype. But setting your hopes too high sets you up for disappointment. Avoid over planning for parties and family gatherings. Instead, find joy in the more trivial aspects of the season: watch a parade with your youngsters or listen to a tape of carols in the car. You'll discover that real joy comes from the simplest sources, and you won't knock yourself out trying to find it.

Refusing to become a Holiday victim, and choosing a peaceful Christmas instead, will not only help your whole family experience more joy and less anxiety during the Holiday season, but teach your children we have alternatives in how we behave. Perhaps as we prepare to once again celebrate the arrival of the Prince of Peace into the world, we can reclaim our own inner peace, and feel truly "joyful and triumphant."

The Value Of Holiday Traditions

Ah, yes...Baking cookies, singing carols, lighting Hannukah candles. Traditions are an integral part of the Holiday season.

Traditions are acts or customs associated with special events, and are repeated year after year. The term originated from the Latin word "tradere" which means "to hand over." Traditions literally hand over knowledge, memories and lore from one generation to the next.

Traditions have played an important historical role in our culture. Their re-enactments have allowed people to periodically relive significant events and to rekindle the emotions associated with them.

Older generations share their experiences with younger ones, bonding them in a common heritage. Young people gain security and a sense of belonging as they participate in the same activities as their great-grandparents.

Traditions enhance current holidays by heightening their significance and emotions. When I attend a live Christmas pageant, I am filled with awe as I experience the events surrounding the birth of Jesus.

Traditions provide guidelines and structure for holidays. They tell us how the celebration will be held. In fact, traditions are often inseparable from the holidays themselves.

The structure of traditions can help minimize stress during the Holiday season. By following established patterns, you'll have fewer decisions to make, and limited options to consider.

Finally, traditions are wonderful vehicles for strengthening family ties. Picking out a tree, attending midnight mass and gathering with friends can help unite families as they worship, share and play together.

To make traditions work best in your family, keep them simple. Don't try to take on too much. Making a simple holiday craft with your young children or attending a performance of The Christmas Carol with your older ones are wonderful seasonal traditions. Perhaps you enjoy reading a passage from the Bible or a favorite holiday tale together. Even the small task of laying out a holiday tablecloth can evolve into a long remembered family custom.

Create positive moods in your traditions. Don't do them when you are harried or over booked. And don't get so wrapped up in a project's details that you can't have a good time. I've seen families come to near blows over whether to buy a flocked or plain Christmas tree, completely forgetting the most important goal is for everyone to have fun.

Emphasize the activity over the end product. It's easy to get caught up in doing something perfectly, making everyone a wreck in the process. Don't fret if your pre-schooler's gingerbread cookies look more like anteaters than people. The time you spent together will be remembered long after the cookies are gone.

Of course, not all family traditions are pleasant ones. People from dysfunctional homes often remember more about holiday drunkenness or disagreements than customs they'd like to pass on.

In such cases, feel free to let go of negative traditions and replace them with new, more positive ones. Think of traditions as guidelines, not straight jackets.

For example, if holiday meals were always spoiled by hurtful jokes about your weight, then boot out the traditional turkey feast in favor of a simple gathering of friends.

You can even start a non-traditional tradition, such as vacationing under the palm trees in Hawaii, or treating yourself to a massage.

However you choose to practice them, remember that loving holiday traditions are a gift you pass on to your family... both your family of today, and those in generations to come.

Surviving Holiday Relatives

The Holidays are here. Time to dust off the ornaments, wrap all those presents and brace yourself for the dreaded nine letter "R"-word--relatives.

Some family members are real treasures. But others are nothing short of pure torture. Aunt Eileen never stops drinking. Brother Bill is out on parole. Dad's new wife is schizophrenic. And Grandpa Elroy never knows where he is.

Still, relatives play an important role in all families. They provide children with a sense of continuity. Grandparents and great-grandparents can pass along family stories and traditions, instilling feelings of rootedness and belonging.

Relatives give kids broader knowledge about who they are and where they have come from. Unfortunately, people caught up in their daily lives often fail to expose their youngsters to their heritage. A family living in a sub-division, for example, may overlook the fact that their forebears were cattle ranchers. Talking and sharing with a wide variety of other members helps fill in these gaps.

Children benefit from any memories they may have of family members. My own great-grandfather died when I was three. But I remember being held up to his hospital bed and having him reach out to touch me. This brief memory has connected me with him and his generation in a way I otherwise would have missed.

Your youngsters can establish relationships with relatives that are separate from the ones you have with those same relatives. Often those bonds are more positive than your own. For example, you may not have gotten along with your father, but that doesn't mean your son can't share warm feelings with his granddad.

Finally, maintaining relationships with the relatives provides a good role model for your children. They learn family is important and, when their times come to orchestrate family gatherings, they will have the motivation and savvy to make them work.

Relatives may have their value, but they can still be tough to get along with.

Keep your expectations realistic. Fantasies about Norman Rockwell reunions usually lead to disappointment and hurt.

Don't get so carried away on the preparations that you're exhausted--and hostile--when the clan arrives. Focus your energies on providing a nice atmosphere rather than a Martha Stewart dining table.

Plan a simple activity to keep everyone occupied. Playing a game, setting up a ping-pong tournament or making popcorn balls give cantankerous family members something to do besides argue.

You may even want to bring out photo albums and encourage Gram and Gramps to share their memories. They'll be teaching the grandkids, while feeling important and providing entertainment.

If you're visiting difficult relatives, set a time limit for how long you will stay. Make the visit short and sweet, rather than long and turturous.

Find something to discuss with those hard-to-get-along-with kin. Ask Uncle Wilmont about the desert tortoises he's breeding, or inquire about Sister-in-law's karate. You may not care at all about these topics, but it will give you something you can share.

Don't forget the value of taking your children to visit elderly and infirm relatives in rest homes and hospitals. It's not always a pleasant activity. But you'll be providing your youngsters with priceless lessons about love, death, responsibility and commitment.

There are only two times I advocate keeping children away from a relative. The first is when they are in physical or emotional danger around the person. The second is when the memories surrounding the family member are so painful that the visit is traumatic for the parent. Under such conditions, find other, loving adults to adopt as family, and begin building new, constructive relationships.

Thank You Notes
A Habit Worth Instilling in Your Youngsters

The Holidays are almost over. But there is still one more important task for our children to complete-- writing thank you notes.

Writing thank you notes is one simple step in the process of teaching our youngsters good manners. Kids learn how to feel comfortable with their appreciation, then properly and graciously express it to another person.

Thank you notes focus children on being grateful for what they have received. Since greed is prevalent this time of year, kids easily fall victim to the "More-More Syndrome." The act of writing thank you notes helps them recognize what others have done for them, and how they can appropriately thank them.

Learning to write thank you notes is a skill that will assist our sons and daughters throughout their lives. Whether they're thanking teachers for writing letters of recommendation, wedding guests for lovely gifts or business associates for helping them in their careers, knowing how to write good thank you notes is essential.

Thank you notes provide a good lesson in language development and composition. First-graders can practice forming their letters and sixth-graders can perfect their letter writing format. Even teens can develop clever yet sincere phrases for expressing their thanks to family members and friends.

Finally, people like getting thank you notes. We all enjoy being recognized for our efforts. And the simple gesture of receiving a card or note makes us feel that our time was well spent.

You can help your kids get into the thank you note habit even before they can write. For example, have your toddler scribble some colorful lines on a sheet of paper, then add a few words of your own: "Tracy says 'Thanks' for her new teddy bear." You can also trace your child's hand on a card, then hold the crayon while you write her name.

As your child matures, she can write her own name on a letter that you have written for her. She won't fully understand what she's doing, but you'll be guiding her toward an important skill.

Assist young writers by talking about what they would like to say, then writing the letter out for them to copy. Keep it short. A sentence or two is all that is necessary for a first- or second-grader.

Older children enjoy writing notes on personalized stationery. Inexpensive paper with their names or initials is a terrific gift to give them, and makes them feel important. You can even buy lined stationery to help keep their sentences straight.

Thank you notes don't have to be a chore. Spread them out over several days, writing one or two at a time. Assist your youngsters as necessary, but avoid getting into battles. And don't expect perfection from your kids' notes. Sincerity--not publication--is the purpose.

Set a good example for your children to follow by writing your own thank you notes to friends and family.

You can even write them to your kids when they give or do something special for you. You'll not only be showing them your appreciation, but you'll be letting them know how nice it feels to get a note.

Don't like certain gifts? It's still important to write and thank the givers. You don't have to be phony. Simply thank them for thinking of you and for their effort in bringing or mailing the items.

Such a letter might read: "Dear Aunt Jean and Uncle Ron, I really appreciate the red sweater you sent me for Christmas. It's always nice to be remembered by family members who are so far away. I hope all is well with you and Grandma. Love, Mary."

Teaching Kids About Giving

As the Holidays approach, and kids add more "I-wants" to their Christmas lists, it's important to provide our youngsters with opportunities to give gifts as well as receive them.

Giving gifts to others serves many functions for children. First off, they learn how to think of the needs and desires of others in their families and communities. Holiday hoopla usually whips them into a self-centered frenzy of the "greedy gimmes." Giving gifts lets them recognize the presence of other people in their lives.

Giving gifts lets children experience the joy and satisfaction giving brings. They get to watch the expressions and hear the appreciative statements of their gifts' recipients. They may receive thank you notes. They learn an important lesson about how it feels to please others they know and love.

Giving gifts allows children a chance to de-emphasize commercialism. Since most of the gifts kids give are homemade, or very inexpensive, they discover that "special" needn't be synonymous with pricey or highly advertised, and that gifts from tiny hands and hearts are often cherished long after other trendy items have gone to garage sales.

What kinds of gifts can your youngsters give? The sky is truly the limit. The best are cheap and simple, and reflect the child's current stage of life.

One idea is making note cards. Purchase blank notes and envelopes from hobby or stationery stores, then allow children to decorate each card in a variety of ways. Youngsters can draw or paint pictures on each card. You can help toddlers and pre-schoolers trace their hand prints with bright felt pens. School-age youngsters can glue their school pictures on the cards. Older kids may want to adhere photographs they have taken.

Help your children write books for those special people in their lives. Young tots can tell you stories, which you write out on sturdy paper, then let them illustrate. Older kids can write and design their own journals or adventures.

Encourage youngsters to write letters to loved ones, sharing special thoughts about those people. We started this tradition last year in our own family. When my son asked what I wanted from him for Christmas, I said a nice note would be fine. The composition I received was so touching and special that it is the only gift I can readily remember. I returned the favor at his next birthday, writing my own sentiments about him.

Have youngsters draw or paint special pictures. Perhaps they can depict a relative's favorite Bible story, or illustrate a well-loved tale.

Make a "Dear Grandma (or Grandpa) Box." Have children write or draw twelve special messages or memories to share with Grandma, then enclose them in a decorated shoe box. At the beginning of every month, she reaches into her box and pulls out one of her grandchildren's notes or treasures. Some may even be dated to ensure she opens them at a specific time of the year.

Prepare yummy food items with kids of almost any age. Boxes of cookies are always appreciated. And don't forget tins of homemade granola, dried fruit, beef jerky, fudge or pasta.

Handy with a sewing machine? How about making festive holiday napkins. Tiny hands can assist in selecting and cutting fabric, while older kids can use the iron or sewing machine.

If homemade isn't in your schedule, take your kids to a local five-and-dime and let them purchase little gifts. They'll be sure to find something just perfect for each person on their list.

Of course, helping youngsters give gifts requires parental time and effort--something we're all short of this time of year. But the joys our children garner from their charitable actions may well be their dearest holiday treasures.

Buying Children's Toys
Shopping Guidelines for Parents and Relatives

Many parents, grandparents and relatives puzzle over the best types of Christmas gifts to buy children. They're not sure if it's politically correct to buy their daughters Barbies. Or they're repulsed by the obscene picture on the skateboard their grandson wants.

Below, I've laid out some guidelines for would-be shoppers for children's toys. These criteria aren't cast in concrete. They're only meant to be suggestions. I don't expect you'll agree with all of them. Rather, I hope you'll be stimulated to carefully consider what you buy your kids.

* Select interactive toys. Interactive toys encourage youngsters to formulate ways of playing with them. They elicit creative, novel responses from kids, rather than dictating to them how they'll be used. Interactive toys help build children's intelligence, ingenuity and imaginations.

Examples of interactive toys are books, sporting equipment, non-mechanized dolls and action figures, games, art supplies, play houses, push toys, tricycles and building sets. Non-interactive toys include video cassettes, video games and all hand-held electronic games. In general, toys that require batteries or outside power sources are not interactive; they work the same way, regardless of who uses them.

* Avoid all violent and vulgar toys. Never buy children tasteless or violent kinds of toys, or clothing espousing

rude or hostile sentiments--even if your kids plead with you to buy them. Just because they want them doesn't mean they get them. As parents, we have implicit authority to oversee our children's possessions, and to help them make good decisions.

Clearly state your feelings about such items to your children. Discuss the social implications of distasteful or aggressive pictures or toys. Then guide your youngsters towards more acceptable and appropriate choices.

* Buy age-appropriate toys. No matter how intelligent your children seem, don't purchase toys that are too advanced or complex for them. Kids need toys that are fun, safe and satisfying. They don't need to be frustrated by lengthy directions, fragile construction, complex pieces or parts they can put in their mouths.

Brad made this mistake when he purchased his four year-old son, Mikey, a remote-control car for Christmas. Mikey loved watching remote-control cars zooming on the sidewalk near their house, and Brad was excited to give him one. But when Mikey opened the box, he grabbed the car and headed for the door, tripping and falling on other boxes as he went. Brad called out, "Be careful. This is expensive and delicate." But Mikey was too busy to hear. Within minutes, he had broken the car's antennae, and had crashed and dented its body on a rock. Clearly, Mikey was too young for such a toy.

* Avoid overly commercialized toys. I know, Lion King and Power Rangers are big hits this year. And most of their products are tasteful and interactive. But I'd like

to see less consumerism directly aimed at children, and more gifts bought on merit rather than merchandizing.

* <u>Select toys that foster social interaction</u>. Toys can provide many opportunities for kids to improve their relations with others. Whether they're building a stable for their plastic horses with their friends, playing catch with the neighbors, or scripting a family produced puppet show, they'll be enhancing their skills of sharing and cooperative interaction. Legos, roller blades, puppets, action figurines and games are all good examples of potentially socially interactive toys.

* <u>Look for gifts with lasting value</u>. Pick toys or activities your children can use and enjoy for years, such as books, globes, games, wagons or sand toys. You'll be supplying your youngsters with long-term enjoyment, as well as teaching them to appreciate the value of well thought out gifts.